John Boyd was born in 1912, the son of a locomotive engine driver, and was brought up in working-class east Belfast. He was educated at 'Inst' (Royal Belfast Academical Institution), Queen's University, Belfast, and Trinity College Dublin. He has worked as a teacher, lecturer and a BBC radio and television producer. On retirement in 1972, he began a new career as a dramatist. Popular success with his play *The Flats* was followed by the publication of his *Collected Plays* Vols I and II by the Blackstaff Press. The first volume of his autobiography, *Out of My Class*, was also published by the Blackstaff Press in 1985. He is currently an honorary director of the Lyric Theatre, Belfast, and edits the literary magazine *Threshold*.

THE
MIDDLE OF MY JOURNEY

JOHN BOYD

THE
BLACKSTAFF
PRESS

BELFAST

ACKNOWLEDGEMENTS

Copyright material from the following is acknowledged:

Louis MacNeice, 'Carrickfergus', *Collected Poems*, Faber and Faber, 1966; W.R. Rodgers, 'The Net', *Europa and the Bull*, Secker and Warburg, 1952. Also, grateful acknowledgement is made to Harriet Sheehy for permission to reproduce a letter from Frank O'Connor to the author.

First published in 1990 by
The Blackstaff Press Limited
3 Galway Park, Dundonald, Belfast BT16 0AN, Northern Ireland
with the assistance of
The Arts Council of Northern Ireland

Typeset by Textflow Services Limited
Printed by The Guernsey Press Company Limited

British Library Cataloguing in Publication Data
Boyd, John *1912*–
The middle of my journey.
1. Biographies. Boyd, John *1912*–
I. Title
822.914
ISBN 0-85640-438-1

Nel mezzo del cammin di nostra vita
mi ritrovai per una selva oscura,
che la diritta via era smarrita.

DANTE

That state is a state of Slavery in which
a man does what he likes to do in his spare time
and in his working time that which is required of him.

ERIC GILL

1

At school I received such an overdose of the life of Julius Caesar that I could never summon up much interest in him later on. I was forced to learn by heart great chunks of Shakespeare's tragedy, which even now I can remember – or bits of them at least – and though I retain affection for the play itself, the stale, chalky atmosphere of Mountpottinger School clings to it. Still, there are few better ways for an initiation into drama, and when I was nine or ten I was glad to know that somebody called Shakespeare had once lived, was exciting to read and had written other plays that maybe some day I would go and see. After I had won a scholarship to the Royal Belfast Academical Institution (Inst) I took every opportunity to act in the annual Shakespeare performances and learned to love *Hamlet*. Nothing but the very best for me, for by this time I had studied A.C. Bradley's book on Shakespearean tragedy and knew what was what. Or thought I did.

Shakespeare's *Julius Caesar* was memorable – no doubt about that. Julius Caesar's own writing in his *De Bello Gallico* was nothing but torture to me – again, no doubt about that. I can imagine no worse choice of a book as an introduction to Latin literature, at least for someone like myself. At the age of eleven I loved adventure stories – Rider Haggard's *King Solomon's Mines* and *Allan Quatermain* held me enthralled – but Caesar's dry-as-dust account of his military exploits left me cold as I struggled through it line by line. Only one sentence survives in my memory, the famous opening: *Gallia est omnis divisa in partes tres.*

I borrow it because though my life is still unfinished, it seems to have fallen neatly enough into three parts. The first – my childhood, upbringing and education – has already been told in *Out of My Class* and ended when I had reached my middle twenties, had graduated and was struggling to find a permanent job as a teacher. When I found one I promptly got married.

Elizabeth and I were married on 11 November 1939, two months after Chamberlain's declaration of war on Hitler's Germany. The brief wedding service took place in the Belfast registry office in Great Victoria Street before half a dozen of our friends. We had high tea in my mother-in-law's house in Madrid Street and then left as soon as we decently could for the village of Ballymacash near Lisburn, where we had rented a small semi-detached bungalow that looked attractive from the outside but soon proved to be cold, damp and uncomfortable.

It was a home and we felt set up for life. My teaching salary in the preparatory department of what was then called Lisburn Intermediate School was £150 a year, the rent of our bungalow ten shillings a week; we furnished the place with cheap furniture, and my books covered some of the damp spots under the front window of the living room. There was nothing to prevent our happiness except the war, and that seemed far away and almost irrelevant.

Life was idyllic. From our long sloping front garden we enjoyed a view of County Down stretching as far as the Mournes, always clear on bright days and obliterated in wet weather; the glittering wintry stars delighted us; we had hills to climb and winding walks down to the River Lagan. Ballymacash itself was a one-street, characterless village inhabited by surly families who eyed us with suspicion as if wondering what a school-teacher and his wife were doing coming to live in a labourer's house. We got a nod and a remark about the weather as we walked to the old iron pump for water twice a day. It was altogether not a very friendly atmosphere. Clearly we did not belong, and just as clearly we did not appear to mind. We were foreigners from Belfast, and if we were Protestants we did not appear to attend any place of worship.

The war continued to be far away and we tried to ignore it, though we often saw British soldiers from Lisburn barracks strolling about the town trying to pick up girls. And of course when Churchill became Prime Minister and the war really began in earnest after the long phoney start we listened eagerly to his broadcasts. Then the American troops appeared on the streets of Belfast looking too well dressed, too well fed, and becoming too popular with the girls, so that we local civilians seemed a weedy bunch compared to these superior specimens of mankind who strolled nonchalantly around Royal Avenue and the City Hall as if they had landed from another planet. We tried to ignore them of course but that was not easy. At one period it was rumoured that conscription might come to Northern Ireland, but the scare passed, much to our relief, and we went on with our civilian jobs. None of my friends had joined up; John Hewitt and Sam Hanna Bell were in civil defence, Roy McFadden was a pacifist and, as for myself, I hated the Nazis and distrusted the British.

I enrolled in civil defence, and that was all. I have such a detestation of violence of any kind that I have never handled a revolver or a gun, and would refuse to do so. If that makes me a

3

physical coward, then that is what I am. But there are millions of us, and if there were more the world would be a safer place. In most matters I am of a sceptical turn of mind. But of one thing I feel certain: militarism is madness. I prefer to think of myself as a coward, and remain sane. I am not an absolute pacifist – or absolute anything – but my life has been such that I have been able to avoid (or evade) violence, and that is simply what I have done.

It would be hard to imagine a more undemanding life than teaching general subjects to small boys and girls in a school of about a hundred pupils. If living in the village of Ballymacash two miles out of Lisburn – not an attractive town – was idyllic, my daily stint of five hours in the company of about a dozen ten-year-olds, if not wholly idyllic, was undeniably pleasant. Boring hours were occasionally unavoidable, but on the whole we kept one another amused and after a couple of years I was given enough senior classes to stimulate my own mind and allow me to communicate to my pupils some of my enthusiasm for literature.

Lisburn Intermediate School was then a small school trying to increase its numbers under the leadership of an amiable science master called Tommy Nunan, who gave the teachers who made up his small staff full rein to teach in their own way. He never interfered, and the standard of teaching – judged by the results in public exams – was high. There was no cramming, just conscientious, sensible teaching, and the intimate atmosphere of the place suited me down to the ground. Elizabeth voluntarily helped with the girls' hockey, I coached rugby and cricket, and between us we knew every pupil. The entire school resembled a large extended family; about half the children were the sons and daughters of shopkeepers and professional people from the town and about half were the children of farmers from the countryside round about. In the mornings they all swarmed through the iron gates and gathered into the biggest classroom for prayers conducted by the headmaster. Only one or two of the staff put in an appearance. The rest of us spent the time chatting in the small classroom which served as a staffroom.

If for some reason Tommy Nunan was unable to take prayers himself he would ask Leslie McCracken, the senior English and history master, to act as his deputy. Although Leslie was a clergyman's son he had little relish for this extra duty and used to swear mildly at the imposition. Once, when both were ill, Tommy sent a message requesting my help. It seemed churlish to refuse but I pleaded conscience and Miss Buchanan, the Latin teacher, stepped in. I thought Tommy should have called on her first as she was the only member of staff who regularly attended prayers, but apparently a young agnostic male was preferable to a middle-aged female believer. Tommy, displeased with my refusal, sulked for a few weeks and withdrew his customary 'Good morning', replacing it with as sour a facial expression as he could muster. But his nature was by no means vindictive and good relations were restored without comment on my churlishness. I do not believe that Tommy himself had religious convictions; for if he had, he kept them to himself. Like most headmasters, he concentrated his life on the smooth running of the school, on keeping the chairman of his Board happy and on cutting as respectable a figure in the town as possible. As his house was an annexe to the main school building he was also *de facto* caretaker whereas his staff, when the final period ended at three o'clock, quickly made their way to the railway or bus station, for they took good care to live in Belfast or Portadown, or in the depths of the country. To my surprise I found that I was an exception in living locally in a workman's bungalow with no mod cons. Being at the bottom of the salary scale, I was not far off the poverty line,

5

but I think I was thought to be living in too humble circumstances. Anyway, at the end of my first year I was granted a bonus of £10, which raised my salary to £160. Riches indeed. Soon we could afford holidays in Ballycastle and Castlerock.

Elizabeth became pregnant and our first child was born in 1941 in the Royal Victoria Hospital, Belfast, during an air raid by the Luftwaffe. It was a bad time for a birth and we fled to Ballymacash as soon as we could. We called the child Deirdre because we liked that pagan Irish name and added Joyce because it would be an alternative if Deirdre preferred it later on, and also because of my admiration for James Joyce who had died in January that year. Elizabeth and Deirdre were well and Ballymacash looked beautiful after the mess of rubble and dirt we had left behind in the city, and the sight of frightened families making for the country. 'FOR KING AND COUNTRY' someone had chalked on a wall in Belfast; beneath it someone else had added: 'YOU'RE FOR THE KING, WE'RE FOR THE COUNTRY'.

2

I have never tried to plan the path my life might take. I thought, if I were lucky, I might become a teacher; and here I was, in a small school, far from the theatres of war, more or less successfully getting boys and girls through their exams and so equipping them better for life. But what life could there be for them? If the Nazi and Fascist forces won the war then civilisation (such as it was) would unquestionably decline – how far nobody knew; barbarism had certainly surfaced in Germany and Italy, and in other countries the outlook was grim. Ireland was still divided, with Eire neutral and the North without conscription. I hated the politics of de Valera with its banning of nearly every author I admired; even more I hated the politics of the North with its intransigent Unionist Party, a party I associated with deceit and reaction. As for the parties of the Left in Ireland, they were hopelessly split and ineffectual. Being a teacher I had hopes that more education would bring more political enlightenment. Because of their class position in society the workers were starved of culture, starved of books, paintings and music. This wholesale deprivation angered me as much as unemployment angered me. And yet when wars broke out, workers bereft of political and economic knowledge were conscripted to take up arms and kill their fellow workers whose ignorance equalled their own. That angered me most of all.

But what on earth could I do to absorb my energies and salve whatever remnants of conscience I still possessed? I thought of myself as a teacher and a writer. Logic dictated that I gain as much experience of teaching as possible, and this was easily arranged. I took an adult class one winter, travelling by train from Lisburn at six o'clock, lecturing for a couple of hours in the Town Hall at Newry, and returning home at midnight to Elizabeth and Deirdre. I enjoyed this class so much that the following winter I repeated my lectures on Irish literature to a smaller class in Lurgan. In Newry my class of about thirty-five students had been enthusiastic: in Lurgan the class was much smaller, fifteen at most, and apathetic. I could not understand at first why the same course could prove to be popular in one town and fall so flat in another. Then, after I gave a lecture on A.E., light dawned. My Lurgan class clearly disliked everything that A.E. stood for, regarded him as a traitor to the Protestant and unionist cause, and were not in the least pleased to learn that such a rebel literary figure was associated by birth with their deeply loyalist community. My suggestion that a plaque should be on display somewhere in the town was received in silence. 'No A.E. here' was the message I got, and I was glad when the course ended.

As I enjoyed talking to adult classes about literature, I hoped that one day I might land a job in the extra-mural department of Queen's university. I never did. In the meantime I was happy enough teaching in Lisburn and making new friends there.

Among the staff at school I was most friendly with Leslie McCracken, a tall, dignified, balding teacher who was about the same age as myself. Leslie's passion was history, particularly

Irish history, and during breaks between classes we used to discuss our futures. We both taught history but I lacked patience for the subject, though I was convinced I taught it well enough. I certainly did not teach it as well as Leslie; he struck me as a born historian and I encouraged him to aim for a university post; he ended his academic career as Professor of History at the New University of Ulster.

Curiously enough, we never became close friends, nor did I ever become close friends with other historians I knew: Jim Beckett or Rodney Green, for instance. Beckett I had known at Inst and at Queen's, but because he had no interest in games or girls I was not drawn to him. During the Second World War he lived for a time somewhere near Lisburn – I do not know where, for I was never invited to his house – and he used to cycle over to Ballymacash for a chat. So did Rodney Green who lived – so I was told – in a large house near Hillsborough, his father being a prosperous grain merchant in Belfast. Rodney was good company, with one of the loudest laughs I have ever heard, and he often laughed. What I liked about him most was his forth-rightness: he was a good hater and his contempt – expressed with a snort and some well-chosen invective followed by a raucous laugh – sometimes made me wonder how he would sum me up in my absence. I remember once asking him about his education.

'Did you like Inst?' I began.

'Aye, it suited me well enough. But it could have been better. Some bloody fools among the staff, I seem to remember. Some good men too, I suppose.'

I admitted I had affection for our old school.

'God, I can't understan' that. I was bored most of the time,' he went on. 'Ye teach yourself, don't ye? Teachers only git in yer way.' Rodney, for all the reputed wealth of his father and his supposedly grand way of living, was a careless speaker and dropped consonants like confetti at a wedding. At that time I think I still suffered from the delusion that the richer your family was, the better your accent must be; Rodney's accent put paid to that notion.

'What about Queen's?' I asked.

'God, I thought we were talkin' about education! That dump! I didn't last long – less than a year!' He gave a snort and made a face as if a bad smell had penetrated the room. 'That bloody place gave me the creeps!'

'What did you study?'

'History, mostly. At least that's what they called the garbage.'

'So did I – for a while.'

I confessed to him that I too had gained little from Queen's and regarded my time there as being largely wasted. Rodney, who was convinced after a term or two that the atmosphere would stifle him, was able to switch to Trinity College Dublin, where the atmosphere was much more to his liking. There he finished with a first-class honours degree. He began his academic career at once in Manchester, then went to the USA and finally returned to Queen's as professor in the Institute of Irish Studies.

When we met, Rodney sometimes took delight in demolishing the reputations of his fellow historians and declaring his enthusiasm for American novelists such as Faulkner and Hemingway. He was especially taken with Faulkner, reluctantly conceding, however, that Faulkner's style was overblown and too much for him.

I had another friend at this time who was devoted to Faulkner's novels: Mr Reuben, who taught maths at Lisburn Intermediate School. A mysterious figure, Mr Reuben joined the staff when the numbers of pupils began to increase. Small and rotund, he had a serene disposition, but was known to be a firm disciplinarian. He socialised little with the staff, but instead concentrated on his teaching, and disappeared promptly in the direction of Lisburn railway station at the end of each school day. Very occasionally, he remained in his classroom with a bundle of exercise books on one desk and his rotund figure squeezed behind another. On one of these occasions he stopped me for a chat. His marking over, he was smoking a cigarette. He confessed that he was trying to give up the habit but without much success so far.

'Would you mind if I asked you a literary question?' he suddenly said.

'Of course not.'

'Would you agree with me that William Faulkner is worth reading?'

'Oh yes.'

'I'm glad to hear that from a teacher of English. Many thanks.'

Mr Reuben then told me of his admiration for Faulkner.

'I don't read much contemporary literature,' he explained. 'I can't really understand why I'm so attracted to this novelist, but I am. Strange, isn't it? You must tell me some day, perhaps.'

No other member of staff had ever asked for my opinion on a literary matter, and this unexpected little chat began our friendship. On the rare occasions when Mr Reuben and I met after school – always in his classroom – he asked my opinion of all sorts of writers, noting down their names in a small worn red notebook. Mr Reuben was about fifty, and therefore old enough to be my father, but middle age sat lightly on him. He had bushy, raven-black hair, lively dark eyes behind his thick glasses, and supple movements, despite his plumpness. Where his lodgings were I never knew – I think he changed them from time to time, but he always avoided staying in Lisburn itself.

11

'Too near the school for my convenience,' he confided in me. 'Don't you find that you and your wife live too near the place?'

'Yes, I think we do.' We talked some more, then I said, 'Would you like to come to visit us? We've a small daughter.'

'So I was told. I'm of an inquisitive nature. Jews are like that, you know.'

I had guessed that Mr Reuben was Jewish even before one of the staff had mentioned his race; I had already made Jewish friends in Belfast, members of the International Club who met in Richmond Lodge, a girls' school on the Malone Road, and I liked them partly because of their intelligence and partly out of sympathy for the persecution that Jews had so often suffered. Mr Reuben clearly was very intelligent but I found him extraordinarily reticent. His first name began with an *H* but I never learned what it was. Nor did I ever learn anything of his academic career, what university he had graduated from, or where he had spent his early life. At the Intermediate School he remained, by his own choice, an outsider; if at that time I had read *Une soirée avec Monsieur Teste*, Mr Reuben would have reminded me of Valéry's eponymous hero, also a mathematician and an outsider. But Mr Teste had a wife: Mr Reuben was a bachelor – at least I think he was, but even of that I was uncertain.

Once, when we were chatting about comparative religion, I mentioned my interest in Judaism.

'Have you ever been in a synagogue?' he enquired.

'Never.'

'Would you like to have the experience?'

'Yes, I would. Is it possible?'

'Why not? There is one in Belfast. I'll take you there one Saturday if it would please you. I find the service rather dull, so I don't often attend. But if you would like to …'

We met at the front of the Great Northern railway station in

12

Great Victoria Street. When I arrived Mr Reuben was already there to greet me, and we made for the synagogue on the Antrim Road. Once inside Mr Reuben donned a little cap which he suddenly produced from the capacious pocket of a long over-coat which made him appear dumpier than normal. All I can now remember of the service was its air of informality and friendliness, with the women in a gallery as lookers-on, a half-hidden, passive chorus. I, too, felt like a looker-on, almost a voyeur, someone who had no right to be present at what was almost a large family gathering.

'Well, what do you think?' Mr Reuben whispered.

'It's all very strange.'

'It's very familiar to me.'

'A lot of talking, isn't there?'

'Praying.'

'Oh, yes.'

'Or else they're talking business,' he added. When he saw the look on my face he gave a chuckle.

If I was an outsider in the synagogue I was fairly certain that Mr Reuben was too, for he never spoke to anyone and at the end of the service we hurried away to catch a bus. When we dismounted he proposed lunch and brought me to a restaurant in Ann Street.

'What would you like to eat? I'm having ham and eggs. It's a very cold day.'

I had the same and began asking questions, more inquisitive than any Jew I had ever met.

When the Abbé Sieyès was asked what he had done during the French Revolution he is supposed to have said, '*J'ai vécu*' ('I survived'). Afterwards he was unable to recall having said this. Perhaps he did not but the sentiment has the ring of truth. Many of us might well have echoed it during the Second World War – or indeed during any war. Anyway, I survived, like the German prisoner I noticed passing by our front garden every Sunday morning. A slightly built man wearing nondescript grey clothes, he walked slowly and listlessly past, until one morning when we were at breakfast I waved at him from our window. He halted, waved back and smiled. A few Sundays later when he appeared on the road I went out to speak to him. Though my German was as poor as his English I managed to convey to him that I would like to invite him in to share our breakfast. After a short hesitation he nodded his agreement and slowly followed me up our rough garden path to meet Elizabeth my wife, and Deirdre, who was then about a year old. Shyly he accepted a slice of bread and a cup of tea, refusing to eat anything more. Not that we had much more to offer, except a boiled egg, for we were on wartime rations like everybody else. But unlike most people, we were able to buy half a dozen fresh eggs occasionally from a neighbouring farm, so on Sunday mornings we sometimes enjoyed the luxury of a real egg each, a welcome change from the substitute powdered variety. But the German gently refused Elizabeth's offer with a sad smile.

He called with us always at about the same time – half past ten – Sunday after Sunday, perhaps a dozen times in all. We talked partly in English, partly in German, with many gestures and misunderstandings. One morning Elizabeth put Deirdre into his arms and he nursed her with great gentleness, glancing from daughter to mother with a look of happiness that mirrored our own. He wrote his name and address for us and we gave him ours. He repeated the name Deirdre and made us understand that such a name for a child was unknown in Germany. We learned too that he was homesick, very homesick for the farm, his father's farm, where he had been brought up and lived before being conscripted into the Wehrmacht. He was a private and a *Kriegsgefangene* in the Lisburn Barracks. I was curious to know more about him, but whether because of his shyness or our difficulty with each other's language I was unable to learn much about his life – except that he was unmarried but would like to marry some day, that he had not yet found a girl, that he loved working on the farm and that he hoped to return home when the war ended. And he was anxious for the dreadful war to end.

We hardly ever referred to the war. To do so seemed inappropriate. But one morning I mentioned Hitler's name.

'*Der Führer*,' he said. By his tone of voice and the glint in his eye I knew he was a Nazi.

'*Nazi Sie selbst?*'

He nodded, unsmiling.

That was the last time he called and we never saw him again. I had hoped he was not a Nazi and perhaps he was not, perhaps it was all a linguistic misunderstanding, but the expression on my face certainly conveyed to him that I had no sympathy at all with the Nazis.

He survived the war and wrote to us as he had promised, thanking us for our kindness to him. I replied. And that was all. Except that the villagers had noted our German's visits and wondered why we had invited him into our house. But we paid no attention to what our neighbours thought of us. Our lives were our own and we were under no obligation to any of the local people.

We did not set out to antagonise them but our behaviour unintentionally appeared to have that effect. One summer evening when I was lying in the front garden dressed only in shorts, reading and enjoying the sun, my peace was interrupted by Lambeg drummers who had halted their procession opposite our house. To listen to two vigorous men in their shirtsleeves beating huge drums only a few yards away was hardly to my taste, so I politely asked them to move on.

'We're not interferin' wi' you – so you've no call t'interfere wi' us,' was the response, accompanied by mutterings of 'Aye, that's right' and 'Min' yer own business, mister.' As I was engaged in preparing lessons for the next day I could have argued that minding my own business was precisely what I was doing and what they had interrupted, but prudence dictated that I should retreat indoors and let the drums deafen our ears until the drummers finally decided to move on down the road, out of sight but not out of hearing.

To register disapproval of Lambeg drummers in a stoutly Protestant village hardly endeared us to our neighbours. Nor did Elizabeth's friendship with the only two Catholic women in the village. Mary, a dark-haired girl from Fermanagh, was the servant in the farm opposite us, and went walking with Elizabeth on her evenings off; so did Mrs Moore, a tall, slim, married woman from County Mayo. The only other friends we made lived about a mile away: the Draynes, too, were Catholics and we enjoyed visiting their farm, where the three Drayne daughters were eager to take Deirdre out of her pram and into their arms. Looking back I find no explanation for these friendships except that in this countryside we felt ourselves to be outsiders – a feeling we must have shared with the Catholics.

Still, we had friends in Lisburn such as Roy McFadden, who worked in a solicitor's office, and Oliver Edwards, a Welshman married to Barbara, a dark-haired beauty who, like her husband, was a linguist. Oliver had been a lecturer in German in Reading, but the whole island of Ireland was his adopted country and he had known W.B. Yeats and written about him. Barbara Hunter – to give her her maiden name – was a Spanish scholar with a particular love for the poetry of Lorca. Together, along with Roy,

16

whose personality and poetry they admired, they often walked to Ballymacash to spend an evening with us. It was the Edwards, I think, who brought John V. Kelleher to meet us and Roy who brought John Manifold, the Australian balladeer, who wore army uniform. What his rank was I never asked; all I remember of John was his rugged good looks and his willingness to quote his own verse at length without self-consciousness, something that Roy would not have done. As for John Kelleher's visit, I imagine it must have been shortly after war had ended; all I remember of John was his friendliness, his courtesy and his stammer. We wondered how he could possibly deliver his Harvard lectures on Irish literature, but I later learned that his speech when lecturing was very much smoother than when he was chatting.

Most of our friends remained in Belfast and it was a relief for us to leave the isolation of Ballymacash for weekend visits to Ballymacarrett where my mother-in-law lived. The fresh air of the country was all very well but I could get too much of it and was glad to return to the stale air of the city. I was city-born and city-bred and more at home there. And I felt completely at home in the McCune house in Madrid Street, off Templemore Avenue, for Baskin Street, where I was born and Chatsworth Street where I had spent my childhood, were only a couple of hundred yards away. I circled round them like a homing pigeon. But my home ground had been battered by German bombs; worst of all, as far as I was concerned, was the destruction of Templemore Avenue public library. When I looked at the shell of the building where I had spent so much of my childhood and youth making literary discoveries, from the adventure tales of G.A. Henty to the masterpieces of Thomas Hardy, I felt that at last I had tangible proof of the barbarism of the Nazis, proof that shocked me more than their infamous burning of the books in Berlin. That was the

17

unresolved contradiction of my life: hatred of Hitler and all that the Nazis stood for, and distrust of the chauvinistic Churchill who now – along with Roosevelt and Stalin – was lauded as one of the defenders of civilisation. And rightly so. But the *Führerprincip* had led to so much bloodshed that I could never stomach it; the 'great man' theory of history made no appeal to me, and in any event self-interest dictated that I survive. I ingloriously followed that dictate in the knowledge that violence was abhorrent to me and that in the thirties, the decade in which I reached manhood, to quote E.M. Forster, 'thousands and thousands of innocent people have been killed, robbed, mutilated, insulted, imprisoned'. The forties were turning those innocent thousands into millions, and no one knew what the future held. All that I knew was that, if possible, I would like to live to see it. Survival was all. So instead of making war I spent the war years in making friends. I might have done better, but I could have done worse.

Among the friends I made was Sam Hanna Bell, who was a couple of years older than myself, and a friend of Bob Davidson. Bob was still in business with Cadbury's and owned a car – so he was a useful friend to have; Sam had a clerical job in civil defence. The three of us had spent holidays at Murlough Bay, where we had the company of Eva Gorstein, who later emigrated to South America, Peggy Lowenthal, who married an Austrian skiing instructor and settled later in Vienna, and Linde Ewalt, who was then a medical student at Queen's and later married Bob Davidson. The Murlough holidays began before war started, and some of our number, including Bob's younger sister Georgie and her husband, an Englishman, kept returning to Murlough year after year long after war was over. Bob, too, was deeply attached to Murlough and when he died his ashes were scattered among the ruins of the old church.

Murlough Bay is one of the most isolated parts of Northern

Ireland. The roomy, sheltered cottage we rented was beside the bay, protected by Torr Head to the south and Fair Head to the north. It was a romantic place, having associations with Roger Casement who, according to the old people, had slept in the cottage and loved to scramble over the scree and along the shore. But the history of Murlough held little interest for me: I was much more concerned with the present. By the present I mean not what was happening in Europe but what was happening to ourselves. We were, of course, escapists from the war raging outside Ireland; and we seldom discussed it. Sometimes we saw convoys of ships in the North Channel on their way to America, but that was all. War was tacitly a *verboten* subject. Eva and Linde, émigrés from Germany, never talked of their experiences there, and certainly none of us ever questioned them about their past. That amazes me now, considering how inquisitive I was. My explanation is that personal relations obsessed us and we gave our attention to little else.

We escaped to Murlough as often as we could, during the summer, at Easter and even at Christmas, and we bathed at all seasons in the cold sea. Adjacent to the cottage lay the tiny beach, sometimes stony but always sandy in summer, when we used the beach most of all. The first summer the German girls surprised us by swimming naked and the rest of us immediately followed their lead. The beauty of the sight of young women running naked in and out of the sea still remains with me as a symbol of our freedom.

At Murlough the sun disappeared early behind the plateau and we spent most evenings in the large kitchen in front of the open fire, reading. The Murlough groups were mostly organised by Bob Davidson, partly because he loved the place and partly because it gave him a chance to be in the company of Linde Ewalt with whom he had fallen in love. The Murlough cottage also gave him a chance to bring his friends together under one roof, for he assumed that people who liked him would like one another.

His instinct was simply to share his friends around. And it worked. I made many lifelong friends in the Murlough days though we were a heterogeneous bunch, with very different backgrounds and interests. Denis Ireland was the oldest member of our group, I think, though he only occasionally joined us. He was then a minor public figure and not at all a popular one, being a Protestant republican and therefore regarded as a traitor to his class and creed. I admired him for his heterodoxy and because the unionists hated him, but I thought his liberalism hopelessly out of date and bourgeois and his advocacy of Major Douglas's Social Credit an intellectual aberration. I had known Denis before his Murlough days (we had met in Campbell's café during the war), indeed I had once asked him to read a novel I had written. He not only read it and approved of it: he also sent it to the Hogarth Press, the publisher of his pamphlet *Ireland Today and Tomorrow*. But we had no luck: John Lehmann returned it with a letter of encouragement, asking to see my next effort. This encouragement buoyed me up for a while: I now believed I had the makings of a novelist and Denis backed up my conviction. We met in his Ulsterville Avenue flat to discuss my literary career but as that did not amount to much, the chat veered to Denis's own career. He had published a biography of Wolfe Tone called *Patriot Adventurer*, a title that would have been suitable for his own autobiography. But he never wrote the full autobiography that he should have written, contenting himself with bits and pieces that are far too fragmentary. He was, I suppose, a journalist, and he certainly delighted in a bout of polemics, but his journalism was much fresher than the usual stuff ladled out by the Belfast newspapers.

Probably Denis was beaten by his environment – the philistinism of the middle class; he has written well of the representatives of this class such as his father, a linen merchant of violent
temper but goodness of heart, who sought perfection in making
linen while his secret ambition was to spend his life at sea. Denis
himself rebelled against the business life he seemed to be destined for, but only after he had given it a try and had travelled for
the family company in Britain, Canada and the USA. With a
wealth of experience behind him, he became an amateur writer,
that is to say he never made a living by his work nor was he
employed by any newspaper. Having a small private income he
could afford to write as he pleased; which is precisely what he
did. He had been a medical student at Queen's, had left his
studies to become a British soldier in the First World War, then
joined the family firm, and finally renounced family, friends and
medicine in order to go his own way. It was in a sense a lonely
way. To renounce (and denounce) unionism in favour of Irish
nationalism required courage from any middle-class Ulster
Protestant; but a renunciation from an ex-captain in the British
Army was tantamount to treason. Denis seemed to be blessed
with a serene temper, however, and of course the safety net of a
private income helped.

At Murlough Bay, and in Campbell's café opposite Belfast's
grandiose City Hall, Denis was often the centre of an admiring
circle who relished his anecdotes. Indeed oral storytelling was
an art that he perfected, perhaps because he spent a good deal of
his time practising it. He loved an audience and told his stories
deftly. Belfast humour greatly appealed to him, but occasionally
one of his stories about the mores of the working class grated on
me. Perhaps I was being too sensitive, too conscious that I myself
was working class and resentful when middle-class raconteurs
raised loud laughs at the accent and attitudes of the class I

21

belonged to. Yet Denis was no snob and, unlike many of his class, made no attempt to overlay his own distinctive Belfast accent with what was our local caricature of an English accent. Like most of us he possessed a streak of vanity, though the form it took was perfectly harmless. He used to tell a story of how once when he was attending the Abbey Theatre someone called out, 'Surely to God that's W.B. Yeats's ghost!' Denis indeed looked remarkably like Yeats: tall and distinguished, with a lock of white hair across his forehead. This resemblance to Ireland's famous poet gave him great pleasure and he was fond of telling that little story. He was equally fond of telling the story of the boxing bout in the Chapel Fields at which the two boxers had exhausted themselves and were resting with their arms entwined around each other's necks until a wag in the crowd shouted, 'Referee, wud ye favour us wi' a song?' I used to attend these bouts myself, as much for the wit displayed by the spectators as for the excitement of the actual contests, but I doubt very much whether Denis ever attended the Chapel Fields. He was more of a collector of stories at second hand, stories remembered to gain the plaudits of the coffee drinkers round the table upstairs in Campbell's where literary aspirants like myself and Sam Hanna Bell congregated.

If Denis resembled Yeats in looks, Sam had a striking resemblance to Bernard Shaw: the same sandy hair, bushy eyebrows, prow-like nose, wide mouth and jutting chin; though many people noticed this resemblance Sam himself never commented on it, at least not in my presence. Indeed I do not remember that he was ever deeply interested in Shaw: Thomas Hardy's novels and stories appealed to him almost to the exclusion of the works of any other great novelist. Though Sam as a young man was certainly interested in literature, he was equally interested in left-wing politics, being an enthusiastic supporter of the Left

Book Club and for a short time the editor of a radical paper, one of the fugitive publications that sprang up in Belfast during the 1930s. We younger people regarded ourselves as Marxists, and few of us ever confessed to finding some of the monthly choices of the Left Book Club indigestible. We had tough stomachs and stout hearts, we were in the vanguard of intellectual life in the city – at least in our own estimation – and we were willing to live for our political faith. To die for it, of course, was quite another matter.

In addition to Denis Ireland, two other older men ruled the roost at Campbell's: Richard Rowley and the painter William Conor. I hardly knew Rowley at all except by sight and was too timid to join his table. I was of course aware of his reputation as a fairly rich businessman who dabbled in literature and had made it known that he was thinking of starting up a local publishing press. As Rowley lived in Newcastle it was to be called The Mourne Press, and when the first three volumes appeared they were heralded as the beginning of a new literary movement in Ulster. Their authors were Richard Rowley, Michael McLaverty and Sam Hanna Bell. Sam's volume was called *Summer Loanen and Other Stories*, Michael's was *The White Mare*. I cannot remember the title of Richard Rowley's book for I never bought it, doubtless out of prejudice, though why I should have been prejudiced against Richard Rowley I have now no idea. Probably it was because I considered him a dilettante, a middle-class littérateur, a prosperous businessman who had no right to be engaged in artistic affairs. I was much more attracted to Conor. Willie made his living by his art, and to do that in Belfast was a feat in itself. He was rumoured to live frugally, and being a modest man he had to be persuaded to mention his own work. Like Denis Ireland, Willie was a good raconteur, and he took special delight in telling stories against himself. I can recall one story he liked to repeat. He was sitting in Victoria Park in east Belfast, his subject the gantries of the Queen's Island shipyard. A group of youngsters stood watching him at work for a while, then becoming bored they left him alone; Willie had politely answered all their questions about painting but he was glad to be shot of them. Standing a short distance away they began an argument about the time. 'You go an' ask that oul' fella,' the smallest one was ordered. Which he did. Willie had to stop working and produce his watch from his breast pocket when the kid came up and said, 'Cud ye tell me the right time, mister?' (In Belfast the children usually ask for the 'right' or the 'correct' time.) After being told the correct time, the youngster turned away and shouted to the others, 'That oul' shite says it's six o'clock!' Willie used to chuckle as he told this story, adding, 'In some places I'm known as an artist, but in Ballymacarrett I'm just an oul' shite!' Willie was not normally given to use such language but the story greatly amused him. So he recorded it accurately, as he recorded Belfast life in his paintings.

With my holidays spent in the cottage at Murlough Bay and my Saturday mornings spent in drinking coffee in Campbells café I found myself in the company of the few people in Belfast actively interested in literature. There were other literary groups and individuals in the city but we paid little attention to them. There was for instance the PEN club, whose meetings I sometimes attended out of curiosity when the lecturer interested me. I never joined PEN, however, as I thought it too genteel a gathering, with too many chatterers. The chat at Campbell's may have been no better, but I was under the illusion – at least for some time – that it was. There was also a group of young writers associated with the publication *The New Northman*; these included Robert Greacen and Roy McFadden, both prolific poets and controversialists who were already making

24

names for themselves in Dublin and London. There was John Hewitt, Keeper of Art at the Museum and Art Gallery, a formidable figure physically and intellectually who attracted a group of his own. I was on the fringe of that group too. Then there was the unseen presence of Forrest Reid, the seldom-seen Michael McLaverty, and the occasionally seen limping figure of F.L. Green.

It was the persuasive tongue of Sam Hanna Bell that brought me, rather reluctantly, to the literary fore. I had no ambition to achieve local fame: having more than my rightful share of youthful arrogance, I regarded Belfast as an incredibly provincial city which could only produce provincial writers of small consequence whose work could not possibly hold any interest for me. My literary standards would not permit me to take any local writer seriously, none being of the first rank. So why be concerned with the third-rate when many of the first-rate writers still had to be read? In Paris in 1935 I had seen and listened to speeches by the foremost European writers, I had brought home volumes by Proust and Gide and Mauriac – not all of them were yet read, of course, but they were waiting to be read; in Ireland itself my standards were set by our four outstanding writers: Shaw, Yeats, O'Casey and Joyce, three of whom had fled their native country. So my literary fastidiousness (or snobbery) made it imperative that I take the local writers I was getting to know not at their own evaluation but at mine. Still, I had enough discretion to keep my literary judgements to myself: that is, until I became editor of *Lagan*.

Sam Bell was adamant that the position should be mine, and Bob Davidson backed him up; my proposal that we should be a troika failed to gain any support. I had little faith in the venture: I was of the opinion that Sam had too much, and Bob, among his virtues, was always agreeable. We started with nothing: no title for our periodical, no money to finance it, no subscribers, no advertisers, no contributions. All these shortfalls seemed to me to be serious obstacles, but Sam disdainfully brushed them all aside. I think he had the notion that if Dublin could produce a lively literary magazine like *The Bell*, we three in Belfast might be able to produce something just as good. Of course such editors of *The Bell* as Frank O'Connor, Peadar O'Donnell and Sean O'Faolain were writers with established reputations, and Dublin was Dublin, undoubtedly the literary centre of Ireland and possessing the inestimable advantage of being at peace with the world. (Though, we in Northern Ireland could hardly claim to be wholehearted supporters of the war effort, as it was called: conscription was never introduced, the reason being that the Catholic third of our population was almost wholly behind Eire's neutrality and the Protestant two-thirds was not as loyal in practice as in theory. Young men such as ourselves were proof of this, though we could plead being in 'reserved occupations': a wide-ranging selection of jobs apparently.) We were of course admirers of the first socialist country in the world, our opinions formed by the Webbs and Bernard Shaw, Palme Dutt and the *Labour Monthly*. But our literary venture shunned political propaganda; we agreed to consider the contributions purely as literature that might be worth reading when the war was over and the world at peace.

We were serious young men and I find it hard now, nearly fifty years later, not to smile when I try to recall what we were setting out to do. We did not succeed, of course, and I never thought we had much of a chance of success; but at least we did not wholly fail. I feel pride now when scholars from America and Germany occasionally ask how and why *Lagan* was published.

Sam provided the title: the River Lagan meanders through Belfast largely unnoticed by its citizens, a muddy, smelly river, especially at low tide. Outside Belfast, however, it runs through some beautiful countryside; its source is in the heart of County Down. It is an insignificant river, though it inspired Forrest Reid to write some pages of evocative prose; that was about the height of its literary fame. Clearly the Lagan awaited its celebrant. Had not Joyce immortalised the Liffey in *Anna Livia Plurabelle*? Anyway we had our title. The three of us put up the cash – £10 each. We supplemented this sum with a few cheap advertisements, found a printer in Lisburn, and the first issue appeared in 1942.

It sold well: the 2000 copies we printed quickly disappeared. Wisely we did not order a reprint, although our success almost went to our heads. I think we must have suffered from delusions of grandeur and I settled comfortably into the editorial chair of what was soon regarded as the best-edited literary periodical ever to be produced in Northern Ireland, the only possible contender for that honour being the long-forgotten *Uladh* published about the beginning of the century. We paid our contributors – Sam insisted on that – to prove that we were professionals; having done that we just about covered our costs. How we were to carry on, Sam never fully explained to me, but he never doubted that we should. It was an act of faith with him, which he promptly communicated to us. I never thought that three professed rationalists could be imbued with so much faith.

Lagan lasted for four issues. Its final edition appeared in 1946, still under my editorship, but with four associate editors: John Hewitt, Roy McFadden, David Kennedy and Jack Loudan. Though it was a good issue it failed to sell even 500 copies. The circulation drop was too steep for us to continue any longer, and anyway I had had enough of editorship.

Perhaps I should mention the contributors to the first issue and to the last. The first issue included work by Michael McLaverty, John Hewitt, Joseph Tomelty, W. R.

Rodgers, Roy McFadden, Patrick Maybin, Robert Greacen, Maurice James Craig, Denis Ireland and David Kennedy. It was an execrable production which somebody likened to a railway timetable, a description that did not worry me overmuch because Joyce's *Ulysses* at its first appearance also resembled a railway timetable, though a much bulkier one. And it contained more errata, but with more excuse.

I was as pleased with the last issue as with the first because it contained two outstanding contributions: 'Armagh: the city set on a hill' by W.R. Rodgers and 'Freehold' by John Hewitt. Only excerpts of Rodgers's radio feature could be printed and it was a pity that the whole script was not available. John Hewitt's long poem with its Wordsworthian echoes is, I think, as fresh now as it was then.

The publication of *Lagan*, and my part in it, was important to me not only at the time but afterwards. Important because it encouraged me to write, and important because it brought me many friends, some of them for life. It may well have brought me enemies among some of the writers of a previous generation whose reputations I rashly (and I now think unfairly) depreciated.

Here, for instance, is a quotation from my first editorial referring to Forrest Reid:

> It may be useful for a young Ulster writer to know what some of his predecessors have accomplished and have failed to accomplish: to know, for instance, that Forrest Reid possesses a good style but has squandered it on tenuous material.

Hardly a judgement, with its self-assumed air of superiority, to endear a distinguished local writer to a fledgling editor, yet it brought me Forrest Reid's friendship.

3

It happened like this. Stephen Gilbert, who was known to be Forrest's protégé, had submitted a short story called 'The Cloud' to *Lagan*, and after some argument among the editors it had been accepted. It was a simply written, imaginative story of a small boy from Belfast exiled to a Scottish preparatory school and feeling very homesick. The story was too slight and too derivative of Forrest Reid's own stories for it to appeal greatly to the editors of *Lagan*. We were all for stories of 'social significance', though what precisely that meant none of us was quite sure, but it was then a fashionable phrase and one frequently on our lips. We agreed that 'The Cloud' was certainly lacking in 'social significance' but accepted it on the grounds that it had style. More important, we did not have the nerve to reject it. Stephen Gilbert had already published his first novel, *The Landslide*, and could therefore be regarded as an established author, which could not be said of many of our contributors. I was surprised to receive a letter from Stephen (whom I had never met) inviting me for a meal at his home in Wandsworth Road and warning me that Forrest Reid might also be present.

At first I felt inclined to invent some excuse for rejecting this invitation. For many years, ever since I had been a schoolboy at Inst, I had read Forrest Reid's books with pleasure, but now my enthusiasm had cooled and something about his writing disturbed, even repelled, me. What that something was I was unable to define. *Peter Waring* I thought to be one of the most sensitive studies of youth and adolescence I had ever read, comparable to Joyce's *A Portrait of the Artist as a Young Man* but not so convincing, not so powerful. On the other hand I found *Uncle Stephen* boring and even slightly distasteful.

So, after my recent unfavourable editorial comment on Reid, I had mixed feelings about meeting the man whom E.M. Forster had praised so highly in *Abinger Harvest*; I remembered that Forster, the contemporary English novelist I most admired, had called *Uncle Stephen* a masterpiece.

Curiosity overcame timidity. I accepted Stephen Gilbert's invitation, and when I met him at his front door and we shook hands, I immediately liked him.

I was nervous, and had spent about twenty minutes walking up and down Wandsworth Road wishing I had refused this invitation. Number 25 was a tall redbrick terraced house with a small front garden, a large middle-class family house which I thought looked forbidding. I was on the point of fleeing more than once, having mentally composed the excuse of a sudden cold, but after vacillating until half past seven I finally summoned up courage to ring the bell. It was quickly answered.

I judged Stephen to be the same age as myself – years later I learned that a fortnight separated our dates of birth – and my first impression of him was of friendliness, of pleasure that I had turned up, and turned up so punctually. He was much taller than I, nearly six feet to my five and a half, straight-backed, boyish-looking, his hair short; he was casually dressed in jacket and flannels. There was the suggestion of a military air about

30

him, though I was unconscious of that until I met him again, after having been told by Forrest that Stephen had served in the British Army and been awarded the Military Medal for bravery before his return to civilian life.

On our first encounter, I have no recollection of our chat during the meal, but I suspect I was gently quizzed about my life as a teacher. And I have no idea what we ate, for I was too busy contributing to the chat and pretending to be at ease. Only when we had left the dining room and gone upstairs to a room Stephen referred to as his 'den' did I have an opportunity to scrutinise Forrest. Like Stephen, he was tall and erect, but my first impression of him was far from favourable. He had an almost square head, with wispy grey hair, a sallow complexion, a wide, thin-lipped mouth and a short, shapeless nose. Altogether he was an ugly man in his late sixties, who wore a nondescript jacket, baggy trousers and a ridiculous little tie more suited to an adolescent. His only remarkable feature was his blue and penetrating eyes, which looked into yours and almost hypnotically compelled your attention.

My ordeal came even more suddenly than I anticipated. We were hardly seated when Forrest, looking stern, went on the attack.

'I understand you referred to my work in your periodical as "tenuous". I've been wondering what you meant. I hardly suppose it was intended to be complimentary. Am I right?'

Although I was used to discussing books and authors with all sorts of people and did not lack confidence when putting forth my opinions, this was a different situation. First, it was two against one (for I assumed that Stephen would be on Forrest's side); second, I knew that Forrest was widely read and was bound to be a formidable opponent; my confidence evaporated. I feared I was in for a verbal thrashing. So when Forrest asked his question I could think of no reply. There was a short, tense silence. Then came my hesitant explanation.

'I meant that your work, in my opinion, had certain limitations.'

'You didn't say that. But surely every writer has limitations? And when you say that, you haven't said much.'

'I suppose not.' I was on the defensive and not relishing the battle ahead.

'You will admit, I suppose, that Jane Austen has certain limitations?'

'Of course.'

'Yet she is considered to be a great writer?' As I could not contradict that statement, I nodded agreement. 'But perhaps you don't care for her work?'

'There are other writers I prefer.' I knew that E.M. Forster was slightly imbecilic about Jane Austen, and that Forrest himself had written an essay on *Persuasion*; so I was crossing a minefield. Stephen sat silent through all this, his head bowed and his eyes shut, almost in an attitude of prayer. Was his prayer on my behalf? Or was he merely embarrassed by what was taking place and regretting his part in it? I had no means of knowing and was conscious only of my discomfiture.

'What other writers do you prefer?'

That was an easy one to answer, and I was relieved that I had been able to divert him away from Jane Austen. I was not particularly interested in her work but I was aware that if I displayed indifference or ignorance I would at once have put myself outside the pale as a self-confessed barbarian. Now I was on safe ground again.

'Tolstoy.'

It was Forrest's turn to pause. 'Why do you regard Tolstoy as a great writer?'

'Because of the range and profundity of his work. He tackles all the important themes.'

'And what are they?'

'War and peace, love and marriage.' The four great themes – all-embracing and monumental – had been tackled head on by Tolstoy out of the richness and complexity of his own life. As I tried to express something of my admiration for the genius of Tolstoy I remembered that Forrest himself had once come under his spell, at least there was evidence of this in *Peter Waring*, Forrest's most realistic novel. I hoped that he would question me about Tolstoy's novels and stories for I was full of them at the time and anxious to talk about them to any listeners I could find. Tolstoy was somebody I could identify with: Jane Austen, being a single woman, and English, and the product of a conventional middle-class society, left me cold. That Tolstoy was an aristocrat did not disturb me in the least. He sided with the peasants, the poor and the oppressed: he was against the rich, the privileged and the powerful. I could not stomach his religiosity and preferred to overlook it. Forrest must have found my thoughts on Tolstoy very stale, but seemed to accept them as genuinely held. He refrained from giving me his own views on the subject. Instead he referred to his own novels.

'And I, for instance, am content – perfectly content – to write about small boys. And small boys are not, of course, as important as grown ups. That couldn't be right, could it?'

His gentle irony failed to amuse me as much as it appeared to amuse him, and I was tempted to answer the question by reminding him that as a teacher I had a good deal of experience of children, if not imaginatively then at least in real life. But I decided against putting forward this argument as I was not wholly convinced of its validity. The truth was that I sometimes found five hours spent in a classroom with small boys and girls day after day just too much for my patience. They could be lovable and detestable, and often they bored me. I preferred to teach older boys and girls, and the nearer they approached adulthood the more interesting I found them. To me, that seemed normal and natural, Forrest's interest abnormal and perverse. Once, when I was still at school, I had read novels like *Pirates of the Spring* and *Spring Song* and been overwhelmed by their beauty. But that was years ago when I myself was an adolescent. Now I was different: I felt more mature than this childish old man who seemed to be living in an imaginative world of his own.

'What experience in adult life do you think important?'

My reply was prompt. 'Marriage.' I felt that this ageing and ugly man, who could never have had an emotional – never mind a sexual – relationship with a woman throughout his adult life, was in his way pathetic. He appeared to me to be sexless and doubtless he then was; I never thought of him as being homosexual. When I mentioned marriage Forrest paused for a while before giving me a reply which I considered feeble. 'My friend Walter de la Mare – who is married – wouldn't agree with you. But then I don't expect you like his work.'

I admitted I did not.

'Have you read *Memoirs of a Midget*?' Stephen asked.

'No, I haven't. I haven't read much de la Mare, only a few of his lyrics.'

'You might like some of his stories,' Stephen said tentatively.

'What novel *do* you admire?' Forrest said.

'*Anna Karenina.*'

'So do I,' Stephen said enthusiastically, adding, 'It is the story of a marriage, isn't it?'

'Among other things,' Forrest said.

Shortly after ten Forrest rose to go, a signal that the evening was over. The three of us went downstairs and stood at the front gate for a few moments. I agreed to accompany Forrest to his home in Ormiston Crescent only a short distance away. We thanked Stephen and bade him good night. Then we walked slowly, speaking only a few words, until we stopped at Number 13 where Forrest lived alone. To my surprise it was a small terraced house. I had expected something much grander. With his hand on the half-open garden gate he turned to me.

'Would you care to visit me some time?'

'Yes, I would, thanks.'

'In the evenings I'm usually at home. Friday is a good evening. But only come if you really wish to.'

I walked slowly back to Madrid Street, content to let the buses go past, mulling over what had happened during the evening. I was certain that I liked Stephen Gilbert, though I was disappointed that he had kept out of the discussion so much; but I decided that he had remained neutral from good manners, from a sense of propriety. How could he take my side when he was Forrest's literary protégé? And how could he take Forrest's side when he knew that Forrest's knowledge of literature far exceeded mine? I suspected that his sense of fairness would not allow him to adopt this course. Still, his anglified accent jarred on me because I thought it affected.

I was relieved that I had not made a fool of myself and flattered that Forrest Reid had invited me to visit him, for rumour had it that he was a difficult person and something of a recluse. In fact, this meeting led to a friendship with Forrest that lasted to his death in 1947, and also to my friendship with Stephen, which still continues.

Elizabeth and I grew dissatisfied with our life in Ballymacash. Because of the increasing damp we had to bring Deirdre's cot into our own bedroom; in cold, wintry weather we went early to bed, sometimes as early as eight o'clock, after having put our feet in the little oven adjoining the fire to take the chill off them. Though I was happy enough in Lisburn Intermediate School I felt the need of a change. So I found a job in the Belfast Royal Academy. I would have preferred Inst, my old school, because I knew some of the staff there and thought I would feel at home. And I owed Inst a lot. But the Royal Academy seemed to me a good alternative and the headmaster, John Darbyshire, had taught me geography at Inst and I got on well with him. Elizabeth and I planned to find a house somewhere in or near Belfast and move out of Ballymacash as soon as possible. But our plan did not work out as easily as we thought. We were unable to find a house to rent, we did not have enough money to put down a deposit for a new house, and so I had to travel by bus to and from Belfast each day. This couple of hours I thought of as a waste of time until I began to pass the morning journey, when my mind was at its freshest, trying to teach myself Greek.

I was disappointed with my new school. My classes were larger that at Lisburn Intermediate and the boys and girls struck me as duller and more lethargic. This was no wonder because I had been given the lowest section in each form and my classes mostly contained children who already considered themselves failures and were at the Academy only because their parents could pay their fees. The boys seemed to have no energy at all, except for an occasional bit of horseplay when my back was turned; the girls seemed half asleep most of the time, except when a couple of them were attracted to a couple of boys, when they would gaze at them with open mouths and follow them along the corridor like sheep. At the end of each day I felt depressed, knowing I was wasting the children's time as well as my own. When the head of the English department asked me how I was settling in, I told him I was bored and objected to teaching the lowest classes all day. A pleasant man and a conscientious teacher himself, he seemed taken aback at my objection, his explanation being that as a new teacher I was at the bottom of each ladder. 'In a few years things will be much better for you. You'll have some good classes then.' But I was not prepared to wait to get satisfaction from my teaching and decided that I would resign as soon as I could.

But before I did I was asked to produce some plays, for the school lacked a drama society and Mr Darbyshire was keen to start one. He remembered that I had acted in the Shakespeare productions at Inst and suggested that I should produce the Academy efforts. He also suggested that *Twelfth Night* should be the first production as it was on the exam syllabus. This seemed to me the worst possible reason for selecting *Twelfth Night*. I argued that the pupils got enough of Shakespeare in school and that to persuade them to give up their leisure to learn Shakespeare by heart was a recipe for making them detest drama in general and Shakespeare in particular. But my argument did not prevail. Parents, staff and pupils were invited to the production which, like all school productions, was described as a success, and I looked like being given the task for ever. If the production had any merit, I imagine it was because I allowed my cast to speak their lines in the way that came most naturally to them. It is not the worst method of producing Shakespeare and I prefer it to some sophisticated professional methods now in fashion.

Of course I had nothing to offer as a producer except my ignorance – and my patience. To see adolescents on the stage for the first – and possibly the last – time in their lives and obviously getting pleasure from the experience gave me pleasure too, something I only seldom and fleetingly experienced in my classrooms. Of course my cast was made up of senior boys and girls – and the most intelligent – so I treated them like the near adults they were, and they generously assumed that because I was a teacher I could teach them the art of acting. I could not; but at least I did not get in their way. And I was not displeased when I discovered that some of the cast took opportunities for falling in love and spending time in one another's company long after rehearsals were over. Despite their enjoyment of this first production, when I asked what play should follow *Twelfth Night* the cast unanimously declared 'Not Shakespeare, sir!' I agreed and asked for suggestions. They had none, but suggested it should be a modern play. After some hesitation the headmaster gave way and suggested a play called *Youth at the Helm*, which he thought a good title and a good play. The cast read it and did not like it. Neither did I. A girl suggested something Irish, so we read *The White-headed Boy* by Lennox Robinson, approved of it, and I produced it. This production also led to a few love affairs. Drama, in my experience, seems to have that effect.

After two years I left the Royal Academy and teaching quite by chance in 1946. Roy McFadden told me he had seen an advertisement in the *Belfast News-Letter* for a job in the local region of the British Broadcasting Corporation and thought I might be interested in applying. The job was for a talks producer, and the salary was £400 a year, nearly double what I was getting as a teacher. Sam Hanna Bell, who had become a BBC features writer and producer, explained to me what the work entailed and hoped that I would join him. Indeed Sam had initiated me into broadcasting some months before when he had asked me to compile a programme of my favourite poems (I forget now which I chose but I remember that they included a new translation I had done of a Lorca poem for which I received an extra

38

guinea). Sam encouraged me by saying that my programme had been well received by his bosses, though who they were I had no idea. At any rate I applied for the job, was interviewed by about six important-looking officials, who went over my *curriculum vitae* and then dismissed me. I had almost forgotten about this interview when Sam informed me there were rumours that over a hundred people had applied for the job; on hearing this I gave up what little hope I had. I was recalled for another interview, however, with only two officials present, held in the office of the Head of Programmes, Mr McMullan, who had been present at the first interview, and his Assistant Head, Miss Eason, whom I was meeting for the first time. They gave me a cup of coffee and asked questions about local writers. I had the impression that they knew little about them, though Miss Eason said she had once met Forrest Reid. Then she asked me if I had read any of the novels written by F.L. Green, who at that time was a prolific novelist, an Englishman living in Belfast.

'Yes, I have.'

'And what do you think of them?'

I paused, wondering what I should reply.

'You know he lives in Belfast?' Mr McMullan said, breaking the silence.

'Yes.'

'You've read *Odd Man Out*, I suppose. It's very popular.'

Yes, I had read *Odd Man Out* and I knew it was popular, but I did not think it had the qualities that give a novel lasting value. I do not know whether or not my self-assurance got me the job, but a few days later I was offered it. A day or two after I had accepted it I ran into my predecessor – his name was J. Nelson Browne – in the Linen Hall Library. Nelson, a small, dapper man, had left a good teaching post in the College of Technology in order to become a BBC talks producer. When I asked him why he had resigned after little more than a year's experience and returned to teaching in the College of Technology he said dryly, 'Are you interested in this BBC job?'

'Yes, I've just been appointed –'

'Not to be talks producer here?' He gave a wry smile.

'Yes. Why did you leave it?'

'I lost a stone and a half within six months.'

'Oh.'

'Of course, you may like it. I couldn't stand it. The strain was too much for my health.'

'I wish I'd spoken to you before I accepted it.'

'You *may* like it. Denis Ireland took it for a while. But it didn't suit him either. Still, it might suit you.'

'You prefer teaching?'

'Very much.'

So the omens were not good, despite Sam Hanna Bell's recommendation. As Denis, Nelson and Sam were all contributors to *Lagan* I was surprised I knew so little about their experience in the BBC; but I think I had little interest in broadcasting at that time, especially from the local 'station'. I came away from my meeting with Nelson Browne feeling I had made a mistake, but when I met Sam he assured me I had not.

Anyway, I consoled myself, if I disliked my new job I could, like Nelson Browne, go back to teaching the young. Like a school or university, the BBC had an educational purpose, and broadcast talks were intended to be informative as well as entertaining, so I conceived my new job to be a kind of adult education job, with speakers lecturing in a studio instead of in a room and to thousands of listeners instead of a couple of dozen. This prospect excited me: I felt I should be in a position of power to mould public opinion; when I was told that I should also be responsible for selecting short stories and poetry to be broadcast, I felt certain

40

that this was exactly the job I wanted. I was determined to make a success of it.

But first of all I had to learn my trade. To do so I was put in the hands of an experienced broadcaster called Horace Fleet, who was a gardening expert and a retired teacher. Mr Fleet, as I called him during my tutelage, was sedate, bald, confident, good-humoured and English. He was an excellent expounder of gardening hints and I listened eagerly to his slightly monotonous voice as he read through scripts to me and Frances Jackson, my secretary, who had to type these drafts before typing the definitive text for broadcasting. Altogether this was a laborious and boring procedure. Then came the excitement. On the day of the broadcast, three hours before transmission, Horace and I would go down the corridor to the small studio with its double doors and its soundproof walls, and there in front of a microphone placed on a table like an icon to be worshipped I was obliged to listen once, twice, thrice and more until Horace almost knew his fifteen-minute talk by heart and so did I. It had been timed by my stop watch to last exactly fourteen minutes and ten seconds; the remaining time would be used by the announcer for his opening and closing announcements. Half an hour before transmission the announcer would appear in the studio, shake hands with Horace, have his voice balanced against Horace's, and then they would sit chatting together, on opposite sides of the table, until the blue light signifying 'rehearsal' changed to red and we were on the air. At least they were: for I would have retired to the adjoining cubicle to join a technician at his panel with dials to be manipulated and a quivering needle to be carefully watched. I would sit by his side, both of us following the broadcast with our scripts, my responsibility being to keep my eye on my stopwatch. If Horace slowed down – and he had been timed minute by minute on the page – we would depress a small key which flashed a red bulb on the table, and his speed of delivery would promptly accelerate. The cardinal crime, I learned, was to allow a talk to overrun its time and be chopped off before it had reached its final sentence. But with an experienced broadcaster like Horace Fleet this never occurred.

I underwent six months of this apprenticeship to the art of broadcasting. It was largely useless, for although Horace did his best for me, the truth was that he himself was an amateur and knew little about the actual production of a broadcast talk beyond the elementary technicalities of timing the script.

Still, the experience of working in Broadcasting House with a comfortable office and a most efficient secretary was such a novelty after the grind of trying to teach none too willing boys and girls in airless classrooms that I began to feel exhilarated, especially after I was released from the tutelage of the well-intentioned Mr Fleet. I also relished the lack of routine and the irregular hours of the job. Sometimes I worked very long hours indeed, arriving in my office at ten o'clock and not leaving the building until so late that I had to run to catch the last train to Lisburn. When this happened I arrived back in Ballymacash tired, but being in my mid-thirties I had plenty of energy. All the same, I was no longer surprised that my predecessor had lost so much weight during his short tenure. I did not lose any weight and was able to absorb the tensions, and as the months passed I enjoyed the job more and more. I was also embued with a good deal of idealism for the principles which the BBC proclaimed it stood for.

When I was appointed in 1946 the BBC in Northern Ireland was opening up after the Second World War and the policy was that more posts as producers should be given to local applicants, Sam Hanna Bell and I being notable newcomers. I knew little about the pre-war history of the station except that some of my friends had a low opinion of it. Forrest Reid, for instance, thought I was foolish when I told him I was giving up teaching. When I asked him why, he answered, 'Your superiors will be inferiors. Anyway I'm sure you are a good teacher.' Forrest, of course, had no idea what kind of teacher I was. All he knew was that I had read Stephen Gilbert's *The Landslide* to one of my classes and his own *Young Tom* to another, and that my pupils had enjoyed both novels and asked for more by the same authors. He himself did not possess a wireless set and his only experience of broadcasting was a series of talks he had given on poetry, addressed to young people. These talks were published later in a book called *The Milk of Paradise*. This experience as a broadcaster had not been a particularly happy one and he never repeated it. He did not believe that I would find much satisfaction in this medium. Anyway, he thought children were often better company than adults, and I had learned not to contradict him on this subject.

The people I met in Broadcasting House were certainly a more mixed and lively bunch than a staffroom of teachers. At eleven every morning the offices were vacated and producers and their secretaries took the lift to the canteen on the top floor, with its wonderful views of the city and its surrounding hills. There they parted, secretaries joining their colleagues, producers joining theirs, and engineers theirs. Round the coffee tables the talk was mostly gossip and chat about programmes past, present and future. The manual staff did not appear in the canteen but took their morning break in odd corners of the building by themselves. Whether they preferred their own company or whether they felt out of place among the better dressed I do not know; at any rate each sought his own kind to drink coffee or tea with, and eat a muffin. Producers often extended the quarter of an hour to half an hour when the chat was good. I liked this leisureliness, which was so different from school where the buzzer or the bell was dictator. At lunch, from one to two o'clock, the tables were more mixed. Afternoon tea was served from a trolley that came round the corridors. Then, from half past five to seven, the canteen was again open, the customers fewer, mostly producers, musicians, announcers, broadcasters. I became an habitué of the canteen, especially in the evenings when most of my programmes were transmitted live.

From the moment you entered Broadcasting House in the morning, greeted by the commissionaire's respectful 'Good morning, sir!', until you left in the evening, greeted by another commissionaire's 'Good night, sir', you were living in a microcosm: everything you wanted was at the end of some corridor or behind some door. If you wanted news you could drift into the news room and lift a paper or listen to the latest 'story' being told by phone; you could wander into a studio where a choir was rehearsing, or into another studio where the cast of a play encircled the microphone, scripts in hand, glancing at one another as they said their lines; or, perhaps best of all, you could relax in the small library looking for ideas by searching through old volumes of the *Radio Times*.

Our small Broadcasting House, modelled after its big brother in Portland Place, London, was a honeycomb of studios, corridors and offices. Your importance could be gauged by the size and furnishing of the office you were given. Mine was on the first floor and spacious, with a table about the size of a billiard table and a leather, soft-cushioned easy chair to curl up in when I felt like withdrawing from the swivel chair that was convenient to the telephone and the green in-and-out tray which the message boys filled and cleared two or three times daily. So, judging by the size of my office, I was clearly somebody of importance. But I soon learned I was not as important as all that. A dull grey worn carpet, no pictures on the wall, no drinks cabinet, no separate office for my secretary – all this meant that I was about halfway up in the hierarchy, with none of the symbols of real importance. And I learned later from one of my superiors that I was given a spacious office only because some of my programmes involved up to half a dozen speakers.

All the same, I felt well cushioned and well looked after; the only drawback was that I had to read scripts to the thump thump thump of my secretary's noisy typewriter. But this I found to be a useful excuse for retiring to the quietness of the library some floors upstairs.

The only other significant object in my office was a huge loudspeaker high up in one corner. By turning a switch I was able to hear what was going on in the various studios, usually rehearsals of one kind or another. Having this loudspeaker was like having a large ear to overhear what my fellow producers were doing and how they were doing it. Later, for some reason I never learned, this facility was removed and rewarded to somebody else. As I did not use it much I was not sorry to see it go. Anyway I disapproved of it and, years later, I became aware of its danger as a kind of bugging device. I was rehearsing a story of Frank O'Connor's and we sat together in the studio chatting after the rehearsal had finished. It was a private conversation, but we forgot it was in a public place. The following morning I was bidden to the Controller's office, warned to be careful what I said while in a studio and summarily dismissed from his office with a reprimand. God knows what I had been saying, or, just as bad, what O'Connor had said. But I learned once and for all that a microphone is a treacherous instrument.

The most enjoyable part of my job was the rehearsals of speakers. All talks by single speakers had to be scripted, approved (and adapted for speech) by me, then initialled for policy by the Head or Assistant Head of Programmes. Many talks were written in stilted language and had to be substantially rewritten. Then the inexperienced broadcaster had to become used to the box-like studio with its soundproofed walls, to its microphone (which seemed to have the power of making even army generals and field marshals tremble at the knees and become tonguetied); and, sometimes most frightening of all, to become accustomed to commands that issued from a terrifying loudspeaker.

To help a speaker deliver his talk clearly and confidently was the producer's aim: and if the speaker succeeded I felt I had succeeded too. Sometimes the pair of us would go to the Elbow Room across the road for a drink and I would be rewarded with a remark like 'I never thought you'd get me through that!' With a cheque in his pocket – for the BBC paid broadcasters at the desk on their way out – and the ordeal safely over, my contributor would be full of the joy of life, like a sprinter who had broken a record.

Within a year, having produced about three talks every week, I began to feel that I had graduated from amateur to professional status. Many of these talks were called 'loose boxes' for some obscure reason and they usually lasted a quarter of an hour. They could be on a wide variety of subjects – travel, folklore, autobiography, history, fishing, any subject of general interest – and they were not considered to be very important in the scheduling of programmes. They were regarded as of 'minority interest' and I wondered if some of them had any listeners at all, for they aroused no reaction even within Broadcasting House. On the other hand, regular weekly talks on special subjects like farming were well planned in series and were eagerly listened to all over Northern Ireland as well as in northern England and southern Scotland. These were called 'service' programmes and the speakers and topics were recommended by an Advisory

Agricultural Committee. To produce these talks I had to simulate an interest I could not possibly feel, being so ignorant of farming that I had never heard of silage or many other important operations.

But I will not dwell on aspects of broadcasting in which I had no interest. Far better to concentrate on the people I enjoyed working with and hasten over the squabbles – not all of them petty – I had with bureaucrats inside the BBC and the bores – mostly local politicians – I had to become acquainted with on current affairs programmes.

Of the dozen local producers I was closest to Sam Hanna Bell. Sam wrote and produced excellent documentary programmes and, equally important, had a gift for nosing out new writers: like Michael J. Murphy, the folklorist, storyteller and playwright; John D. Stewart, a man of many talents; and Sam Thompson, the shipyard worker who wrote *Over the Bridge* which was considered too controversial a play for the Group Theatre and the BBC. These three writers – and many others, of course – contributed to talks as well as to features. Sam and I were constantly exchanging ideas and trying to liberalise what we considered was the narrow parochialism of the region. Sometimes our ideas were thought to be unacceptable, and when this happened we shared our frustration by leaving our offices in the early afternoon and seeking refuge in the Elbow Room to lick our wounds. Sam had a bohemian streak that I found congenial. Indeed it was a streak endemic in the whole features department, and producers like Louis MacNeice and Bertie Rodgers in London seemed to spend as much time in the pubs around Portland Place as they did in their offices in Broadcasting House. It was not wasted time either in London or in Belfast and, to be fair to the upper echelons of the BBC hierarchy, at least some of them had a notion that drinking had

47

to be secretly condoned as something mysteriously connected with the creative process. In the London talks department, by way of contrast, I found there was a pervasive atmosphere of civil-service sobriety which drove a few of us into pubs in search of our colleagues in features.

I sometimes had the feeling I was in the wrong department.

4

In the years immediately after the Second World War the housing shortage was acute and Elizabeth and I still were unable to
save enough money to put down a deposit for a house of our
own. So for a couple of years more we had to endure the discom-
forts of our bungalow in Ballymacash. When Roy McFadden
came to visit us he liked to leaf through the bookshelves beneath
the warped, draughty front windows. These bookshelves gave
the room an air of being lived in, and also covered damp spots
where the wallpaper was hanging loose. On one occasion he was
leafing through a biography of Zola, which I remember I had
found unreadable.

'Look what I've found!' he said, holding up some pound
notes.

'How much have we saved now?' I asked Elizabeth.

'Twenty pounds.'

'Why do you hide it in the Zola?' Roy enquired.

'Because that book isn't worth reading,' I said. 'No one will
steal it.'

That twenty pounds was our savings and was destined to be
spent on our Easter holidays. It amused Roy greatly that we

should put our savings in a book for safety, but we could think of no more secure place. Though we lived simply we seemed to be unable to save, probably because I was fond of buying books and we liked to take holidays as often as possible.

Determined to find accommodation in Belfast, at last we found it, though it was not exactly what we wanted. Unable to afford a house, we found a roomy flat above a doctor's surgery in Templemore Avenue. We had the first and second floors with plenty of space for furniture and books, and a spare room for my brother Jim, who was then a reporter on the *Northern Whig*. We were fond of Jim – I never met or heard of anybody who was not – and we were glad of his company; our daughter Deirdre was probably the best audience he ever had for his violin-playing, which was more enthusiastic than skilful; wide-eyed and wondering, she gave him all her attention. He may have had other admirers of his art but they were unknown to us, and he always practised in his bedroom, a thoughtful act typical of his nature.

Instead of paying rent for the flat we had to pay for a cleaning woman who washed the surgery out twice a week, Elizabeth keeping it tidy on the other days; we also had to take calls every evening from Monday to Friday and all day on Saturday and Sunday. So the doctor got his money's worth from us, and with no rent to pay we were able to save at last. But we did not intend to prolong our stay in the flat.

The biggest disadvantage were the frequent night calls, which nearly always came when we had just fallen into a deep sleep; Elizabeth or I had to grab the phone, take the message – which was usually given by a distracted patient pleading for the doctor to come out at once – then we had to ring for the doctor, repeat the message as well as we could (for he too had to be rudely awakened) and endure his irritation as he tried to make up his mind whether the call necessitated his leaving his warm bed or whether he could take a chance and go back to sleep. He was a conscientious doctor but short-tempered, and when we relayed the substance of the call he seemed to expect from us a prognosis of the case. Afterwards, if it was a pregnancy Elizabeth and I would discuss its urgency, wondering whether the doctor had answered the call.

'Are you still awake?' Elizabeth would whisper.

'Of course I am.' My irritability now more than matched the doctor's.

'I wonder did he decide to go out?'

'How do I know?'

'I'm just wondering.'

'Don't! Go asleep!'

'I can't. The sleep's left me. What time is it?'

'I don't know and don't care!'

'It's not a very nice night to be called out, is it?'

Having no interest in the weather I saw no need for a reply. I hated these nocturnal exchanges and groaned my displeasure, suppressing the curse on my lips and furious that Elizabeth should be concerned and upset with something that was not our responsibility.

After the evening surgery when the doctor had gone home and the front door had been closed the bell sometimes rang and a patient stood on the step demanding treatment for a burn or a dislocated bone. On these occasions I was sometimes mistaken for the doctor and found it hard to persuade the patient that I was ignorant of medicine and was only the caretaker. One evening a young woman arrived in great distress and I brought her into the surgery. Before I could speak she burst into tears.

'Doctor, you'll have to do something for me quick!'

'But I'm not – '

Before I could say who I was she had lifted up her dress. 'Look, doctor, I'm bleedin' to death. I'm goin' t' die if you don't stop it!'

'All right ... all right. I'll phone for the doctor. He's just left. I don't know whether he'll have arrived home yet. Lie down please. Over here ...' I got her onto the doctor's black leather couch with a little difficulty for she was plump and clearly pregnant.

'What'll I do? What'll I do if he doesn't come soon? You're a doctor, aren't you? You look like a doctor. Can't *you* help me?'

I tried to explain who I was, but the young woman seemed incapable of understanding what I was saying, convinced in her own mind that I *was* a doctor, who for some reason was refusing to help her. The phone was engaged and I could not get through, so I tried to calm her down, telling here there was no danger of her dying (though I was not at all sure about that).

'What happened?'

'I interfered with myself, doctor. I shouldn't have. It was wrong, I know ... I know that ... And I want my baby ... Honest I do ... I won't lose it, will I? Tell me, will I? And I won't die, will I? God is good, isn't he? He'll forgive me, won't he?'

I assured my patient – for now I regarded her as such – that God would forgive her and that the doctor would certainly come to her help. In the meantime, if I failed to get him on the phone I would ring the hospital. So she had no need to worry.

At my third attempt I got the doctor's number and his wife answered. She promised to tell him immediately he came in – she was expecting him any moment. All we could do was wait. The young woman – I had not asked her name and address – lay huddled on the couch, and though I had put on the small electric heater the surgery was cold and she was shivering. I gave her a grey blanket from the cupboard to cover herself up but she shook her head.

'He won't be that long, will he?'

'No, I don't think so.' I sat on the doctor's chair in front of his rolltop desk and wished that I was really the doctor. 'Would you like a cup of tea?'

She shook her head. 'Will the doctor be long?' She was snivelling now, her handkerchief a small wet ball in her clenched fist. I gave her my own handkerchief, which was grubby enough but better than her own and she sniffed her thanks. I had time to look at her now. She was plain and dumpy, about seventeen, with blotchy skin and eyes swollen with crying. 'The doctor'll be cross wi' me, won't he?'

I reassured her but did not know what else to say, just feeling something of a fool and an impostor. Once I stood up from the chair and made to leave the room but she asked me where I was going to, her eyes so pitiful that I sat down again. I had only intended going upstairs to tell Elizabeth what was keeping me and to ask her to come down. A woman would be better with another woman. I was useless and becoming worried, blasting the doctor for taking so long. Then I heard the door open and his step in the hall. He entered the room.

'What's this? What's all this?' he said, a crabbed look on his face.

'*Your* patient, doctor.'

He thanked me but in such a way that he need not have bothered. I never enquired afterwards what had happened.

Despite many interruptions to our life – the phone ringing at all hours and the patients calling between surgeries – we were glad to be free of the bungalow in Ballymacash and thankful to be installed in Belfast. We missed our view of the County Down landscape to the Mournes in the far south and, in the north, beyond our back garden, the fields rising to the Antrim Hills that stretched all the way to Belfast. We missed the fresh air and the morning birds and the quiet nights. But the flat had compensatory comforts even if we were only caretakers in a house we neither owned nor rented. Elizabeth's parents lived only two minutes' walk away in Madrid Street; my father's brother and sister lived in Portallo Street off the Castlereagh Road; and in Ardenlee Avenue there were my sister and her husband. So we felt we belonged to Ballymacarrett and it was a good feeling to have. I suppose this is an atavistic instinct and therefore powerful and permanent. With time you may be able to distance yourself from the place of your childhood, but you cannot eradicate it, scrub it out of your memory, rid yourself of its sounds, sights and smells: the weathered brick of narrow streets; the proliferation of little shops on the Newtownards Road and the Albertbridge Road that you could never pass without peering into; the churches of all shapes and sizes at almost every corner; and, most mysterious of all, the Roman Catholic chapel which you hurried past, afraid to lift your head because you were now in enemy territory and your very life was in danger.

That I should have returned to live so near the place of my birth and childhood astonishes me now, and I cannot help wondering whether I possessed an overdose of the homing instinct displayed by the pigeons which landed safely from Bordeaux or Penzance into their lofts in the backyards of Chatsworth Street. This miraculous feat has always stuck glue-like in my mind and I remember the sense of disappointment I had as a boy when my father showed no interest in homing pigeons, calling them dirty birds that made a mess, which meant that I would have to be content with sitting on top of our yard wall to view the long-distance homers coming home, first one, then another, then another, all hesitating for a moment on the ledge of the loft before triumphantly disappearing inside.

Yet I cannot now admit to a feeling of nostalgia for Ballymacarrett, even though when I was growing up it satisfied all my needs. For then I was hardly aware of its ugliness, its air of squalor and staleness, the sour stench from the River Lagan at low tide in summer, the acrid stench from the fertiliser factory on the Mountpottinger Road, the nauseating slime of the Connswater river meandering its way past the ropewalks towards the shipyards and Belfast Lough. I suppose a boy accepts his environment as he accepts nature; his aesthetic sense lies dormant until he is capable of making comparisons: ugliness is not ugliness until beauty has been experienced. Anyway, I felt lucky to be living in such a lively and crowded place, with contortionists and ventriloquists and knife-throwers in the Popular cinema, and cowboy films in the New Princess; even the drab Willowfield cinema on the Woodstock Road had its attraction: its one-armed guardian who waved his stick if you dared to climb out of your seat or yell at the frightening episodes of the big picture.

And now I had returned to Ballymacarrett as a married man with a daughter ready for school, and the only convenient one was Mountpottinger Elementary, which I had detested but from whose discipline I had benefited to gain a scholarship. So we sent Deirdre to Mountpottinger girls school, but determined to withdraw her at once if she were unhappy there.

In Ballymacarrett Elizabeth and I were back to where we were born and brought up, but with a big difference. Instead of being a thin, undersized kid with a passion for collecting books of all sorts and playing football with a hankie ball and cricket with a homemade bat, I had collected three degrees from two universities, achieved my ambition of becoming a teacher of English and history, then, having become disillusioned with teaching, had by a fluke found myself inside the 'Establishment' of the BBC. The fluke was that I had been one of the three founders of a literary periodical started without any notion of profit but simply because we thought it worthwhile for its own sake. Without the unexpected success of *Lagan*, I do not believe I would have landed the BBC job. *Lagan* may have helped Sam to get his job too, for Louis MacNeice had a hand in that, and Louis had contributed to *Lagan*.

The restriction in my new work that irked me most was in the field of literature, and particularly affected the broadcasting of short stories. The policy was to cultivate our own garden, that is, to concentrate attention on short-story writers from the Six Counties. This policy was, of course, understandable from a political point of view: the BBC existed in Northern Ireland to serve the broadcasting needs of the Northern Irish population. (The word 'Ulster' was given widespread usage in an attempt to make it acceptable – a piece of linguistic sleight of hand that the Catholic minority found offensive, as did some Protestants such as myself, our Ulster being the historical province of the north and not the six counties of the north east as truncated by the artificial and arbitrary political border.) Because Ireland had been divided into two parts, though only as recently as the third decade of the twentieth century, the BBC governors in London seemed to imagine that Irish literature could suddenly be sliced up like ham to suit the political needs and appetites of the time. This stupidity, which was not confined to London, had the backing of Belfast. It was one of the cultural effects of partition.

I found it impossible to stomach. Of course it was right to broadcast the stories of Michael McLaverty, Joseph Tomelty, Brian Friel, Sam Hanna Bell, John O'Connor, Lynn Doyle and a few more, but what justification, other than political, could be advanced for ignoring the rich tradition of short-story writing throughout the whole island of Ireland? It was a form of literary apartheid and like all apartheid it was ugly and ultimately unworkable. There were simply not enough good writers in the North to satisfy the needs of the BBC; just as there were simply not enough dramatists or poets. So in my first two years as a producer I began to put forward arguments for ridding the region of its literary exclusiveness, citing the example of music. In the music department, programmes were in the hands of two Dubliners – Edgar Boucher and Havelock Nelson – whose wide and deep musical knowledge allowed them to exercise a degree of artistic freedom denied to producers like myself whose concern was with the spoken word. I envied the musicians and hoped I could find a way to follow their practice. The constraints on literary policy I found intolerably narrow, being regional and sub-national; the only way out of the impasse was to protest that such a policy was impractical.

I began my protest by inviting Frank O'Connor, the Irish short-story writer I most admired, to broadcast from Belfast. This I remember as my first successful dent in the literary parochialism I found so stifling. I had already heard O'Connor broadcast one of his stories from London and was so impressed that I wrote asking him would he be willing to come to Belfast. He replied at once that he would be delighted. And our friendship began.

You either loved or hated O'Connor: it was impossible to be indifferent to him. From our first meeting I grew to love him, and when I saw him on the platform of the Great Northern station coming from the Dublin train I recognised him at once – his head tilted as if to see better through his glasses, his tweed hat in one hand and a small bag in the other, and his gait of someone with plenty of time on his hands and not a care in the world. I did not

57

know it then but he in fact had more than his share of worries. But his nonchalant air and his quizzical look as if to say 'Well now, I wonder what's going to happen here?' belonged to a man at ease with life. As he reached the ticket collector's gate I addressed him even before he had shown his ticket.

'Frank O'Connor?'

He halted, taken aback at the sound of his name, for I had not warned him that I would be at the station to meet him. 'Yes.'

I introduced myself and his face creased into a grin as we shook hands.

'I didn't think I was going to be met,' he said, still smiling, 'except by a detective, perhaps.'

I let the cryptic remark pass, though I wondered what scrape O'Connor had got himself into, but decided that it was just a joke to break the ice. Later I discovered that he was not joking at all.

After the broadcast he came to our Templemore Avenue flat. I think he was our first guest. I remember his mild disapproval when I told him how I had returned to live in the little area of Belfast where I had been brought up.

'I couldn't live in Cork,' he said. 'I had to clear out as soon as I could.'

'You don't like your native town?'

'Oh, I love it,' he growled in his sonorous Cork accent. 'I love it. But I couldn't live in it. Impossible!' He explained that as an idealistic and rebellious young man, he had been driven almost mad there and had escaped to preserve his sanity. He imagined I would feel something the same about Belfast. If so, I should clear out while the going was good. But maybe, he added, Belfast was not as bad as Cork.

When I accepted a job in the BBC I did not know what I was letting myself in for. I soon realised that though the pay was good and the life pleasantly varied, it was a job that absorbed my energies and left me with no spare time. Or very little. When I was teaching I had had time to edit *Lagan*, time to read, time to write an occasional story, essay or poem. I published hardly anything, but a poem in the *Irish Times* or an essay in the *Dublin Magazine* were enough to give me hope that some day I might really write something worthwhile, that is, given time. But now time was being filched away from me, and I was told that it would be impossible for me to continue editing *Lagan*. As this had taken up only a small part of my spare time when teaching – and was a non-profitable pursuit – I took a jaundiced view of the situation. I could not accept that an employer – *any* employer – had the right to take over my whole life. It was too precious for that. The fact that *Lagan* had run its course and I had no desire to go on with it was irrelevant. If teaching did not curtail my personal liberty to the extent of preventing me from running a literary periodical, I could see no reason why broadcasting should. But it did. Also, having completed an extramural B.Litt. thesis at Trinity College Dublin on Forrest Reid, I was advised not to continue with a book on Reid which I had begun and which H.O. White, my Trinity professor, was encouraging me to complete. This negative, bureaucratic attitude seemed to me stupid and repressive and I had a suspicion that it was unique to the Northern Ireland region. In London members of the BBC staff like Louis MacNeice or W.R. Rodgers could continue with their own writing in addition to their radio work: that caused no problems there. So why should it here? But an outward show of rebellion was not feasible so I had to swallow my bile. Still, I never convinced myself that Forrest Reid was right when he advised me to remain a teacher.

When I got to know Forrest he was in the last years of his life, his best work had been done and his health was in a slow decline.

They were not happy years, for he was suffering from mysterious pains in his back and his thoughts sometimes turned to death. He made no complaints, at least to me, and whenever he mentioned death – and this was seldom – he appeared calmly reconciled to it. Perhaps Socrates was not too far from his mind. Forrest was not a Christian, and had no belief in an afterlife.

After that first contretemps in Stephen Gilbert's house I received nothing but kindness from Forrest. I visited him usually on a Friday or Saturday evening, arriving at about eight o'clock and leaving at about ten. Usually I found him alone, sitting in his chair and smoking his pipe. Sometimes, but not often, he would be reading or playing patience.

The front room of 13 Ormiston Crescent was small, but neat and tidy except for the hearth, where a small coal fire burned in winter; in summer, when the fire was out the hearth looked neglected. On one occasion I picked up a pile of paper that he intended to use for lighting the fire should the weather turn cold, and I found that the typed sheets comprised a handwritten, corrected typescript of his little anthology of poetry called *The Milk of Paradise*.

'Are you proposing to burn this?' I asked, amazed, for I was well aware that he loved collecting books and stamps, indeed anything that took his fancy.

'I've no use for it,' he replied, amused at my amazement.

'May I have it?'

'Of course. You had better see that all the pages are there,' he said, the collector in him coming to the fore.

All the pages *were* there and I took them home to be bound. It was a gift I prized more than the inscribed book itself, which he gave to me on its publication. 'You may like one or two of the poems,' he said on that occasion, his eyes glinting mischievously behind his glasses. He drew his forefinger across his wide mouth in an attempt to hide his smile. For he knew that our taste in poetry differed widely, and knew too that argument on such a matter was a waste of breath. But he was right: there were a few poems in his little collection that I did like – those by Blake and Wordsworth for instance – but in general I thought Forrest's taste was too narrow and sentimental: it lacked humour and earthiness and bite. The gap in years and temperament proved far too great to be crossed. So, wisely, we did not try but instead accepted our differences. After all, we had a good deal in common, especially in prose. We both loved Turgenev, Flaubert, Mark Twain and Hardy, and they were certainly enough to keep us talking for years.

In the last decade of his life Forrest was lonely: of that I have no doubt. The Second World War had cut him off from visiting English friends like E.M. Forster and Walter de la Mare and of course from attending operas at Covent Garden; at home his circle of friends had grown smaller. Stephen Gilbert looked like getting married, an event that Forrest took no pleasure in contemplating, George Buchanan was serving in the RAF abroad, and some old Belfast friends had died. He had made new friends, like Robin Perry, an aspiring writer from Bangor, and an intelligent young woman called Doreen Sheridan who like Forrest himself had been to Cambridge, and who now worked as a BBC executive. I think neither Robin nor Doreen liked me very much, at least that was my impression, though Robin once let me read a novel he had written about the goings-on of a group of adolescents in Bangor; I praised it, thought it deserved to be published, but it never was. What Forrest thought of it I never learned. Anyhow Robin, a tall thin intense young man who seldom smiled and seemed to lack energy, eventually became a journalist in Belfast and died comparatively young, a writer *manqué*.

I was something of a writer *manqué* myself and could well sympathise with Robin. Doreen was, I imagine, slightly younger than myself: a cool attractive woman with a slim figure, well-cut features and an English accent. She was unique among Forrest's friends in being young, attractive and a woman. She certainly never flirted with him (if that were possible), nor with me (and that *was* possible), nor with Stephen (and Forrest would almost have approved of that). But Stephen had made up his own mind whom he would marry, and did; when his marriage took place, Forrest found it hard to forgive. Like myself, Stephen was very independently minded, which is one of the reasons we became friends. With him and George Buchanan I could cross what appeared to be a class barrier; with Robin and Doreen I failed.

Usually I saw Forrest alone, for this was the best way to enjoy his company. We did little but talk, and there always seemed plenty to talk about. His was a writer's front room, full of books; when there was a lull in our conversation I would take a book down from the shelves and ask about it and its author. Being a collector Forrest was reluctant to lend his books except to his closest friends, and there were certain sets, such as his collection of Henry James, that were sacrosanct. As I wanted to own a set of Forrest's work he presented me with *Spring Song* and *At the Door of the Gate*, novels long out of print. But what gave me more pleasure than these gifts was the letter he wrote asking my help with the proofreading of *Young Tom*. This letter ended with the sentence, 'I'll do the same for you when the time comes.' That was Forrest's way of saying 'I believe you are a writer', and it was music in my ears. It gave me the confidence in my writing I so badly needed.

In E.M.Forster's opinion Forrest was the most important person in Belfast. This was an opinion I shared and I was not likely to forget that it was a privilege to belong to his small circle. I did not know all of his friends of course, and one I disapproved of. This was Knox Cunningham, to whom he had dedicated *The Retreat* and whose political opinions I detested. Knox was a prominent Tory Member of Parliament at Westminster, a unionist and an advocate of capital punishment; his friendship with Forrest I found incomprehensible. I wondered what a liberal like Forster would have thought of it, and imagined that he would have little time for such a reactionary as Knox. Tolerance could be stretched too far I believed, and when Forrest spoke kindly of Knox I was not amused. Nor was I amused when he told me that he would like to arrange a meeting between us.

'What have you in common with Knox?' I asked him.

'He likes my books,' he replied. 'And we talk about stamps. Knox has a very good collection.'

'Why don't the pair of you grow up?' was the comment I should have liked to make but did not. It might well have ended our friendship.

'Why would you like us to meet?' I asked.

'To listen to you both argue about politics.'

'But I'm a socialist and Knox is a reactionary even among Tories. We have nothing in common. We would have a row.'

One Friday evening when I arrived at Forrest's, Knox was already there, whether by accident or design I do not know. A tall, well-built, smiling man with what I thought (prejudicially, no doubt) a baby-like face, Knox greeted me with a hearty handshake, the kind of handshake that politicians distribute wholesale during election campaigns. 'Forrest has told me about you,' he began, 'and I'm very glad to meet you.' When we sat down Knox again addressed me. 'Are you interested in stamps?'

'No.'

'I mean collecting stamps – rare ones preferably.'

I admitted I had no interest at all in stamp-collecting.

'I think you disapprove,' Forrest said, an impish expression on his face, as if daring me to voice my disapproval.

'I neither approve nor disapprove.'

'Well, I think you do disapprove,' he added.

'*Chacun à son goût*,' Knox said with a tolerant smile. 'You once told me, Forrest, that Forster disapproved of your collecting habits.'

'That's right.'

'So you're in good company,' Knox said to me, smiling. 'I believe you're interested in sport.'

I admitted that I used to play rugby and cricket.

'Knox was a champion boxer at Cambridge,' Forrest announced, as if proud to be in such august company, or maybe he was legpulling – I failed to decide which. Then I remembered that Forrest himself had been a champion croquet player, a game I had never seen played and associated with the lawns of large country houses.

The chat veered away from sport and reverted to stamp-collecting until Knox suddenly rose and announced he had to leave. Forrest asked me to stay on a while, which I did, hoping that the evening would not be entirely wasted. When Forrest returned to the room, having shown Knox to the gate, I must have looked a little sullen.

'Well, what do you make of Knox?'

'He seems very pleasant,' I managed to say. But for me the evening was irretrievably lost and I left earlier than usual, consoling myself that at least politics had not come up for discussion.

When Forrest and I did discuss politics some months afterwards I initiated it. Unable to accept with equanimity his complete ignorance of social problems whether local, national or international, and irritated by his complacency about that ignorance, as if it were a virtue and not a defect, I took it into my head to arouse him out of his lifelong political apathy by lending him the first book on politics I myself had ever read: Bernard Shaw's *An Intelligent Woman's Guide to Socialism*. I chose the right moment to lend him this book, for a local election was due and my plan was to persuade him to vote for the Labour candidate. Only once before had I tried to talk politics to him, but his look of boredom on that occasion made me give up the effort; now I had hit on the idea of getting Shaw to do the persuasion for me.

'Will you promise to read it?' I cajoled him.

'No, I won't promise.'

'But you like Shaw's plays, don't you?' I had noticed, to my surprise, three or four volumes by Shaw among his shelves and knew he must have read them, otherwise he would not have kept them.

'Yes,' he grudgingly admitted. 'At least I like some. Not many. One or two.'

'You admit he writes well?'

'Oh yes, very clearly. He has a style all of his own. Not the kind of style I'm fondest of. Yes, I'll try to read this book. It's very long, isn't it? I mightn't be able to get through it all!' I had little faith that my strategy would work.

A fortnight later when I called at Number 13 Forrest must have seen me at the gate, for he hurried down the hall to greet me; he appeared at the front door grinning and clearly in a happy frame of mind. Without giving me time to speak he blurted out, 'I'm a socialist!'

'What on earth do you mean?'

'I tell you – I'm a socialist. I've read your book – I mean Bernard Shaw's book – and he has converted me. I can't see a flaw in his argument.'

I followed Forrest up the hall and into his room, so flabbergasted that I was out of breath. Forrest looked at me, a grin still on his face. 'You look very surprised,' he said, staring with his eyes wide open, a habit he adopted when he wanted all of your attention.

'I *am* surprised!'

'I thought you would be. But Shaw's argument is only common sense, isn't it?'

I could not refrain from showing off my knowledge of Shaw's works by telling Forrest that an earlier book by Shaw was actually called *Common Sense about the War*. But Forrest showed no interest in the earlier book – the one that he promptly returned to me had given him enough to think about.

I put on my superior air. 'I'm glad you liked the Shaw. It is of course open to criticism. Fabianism is now out of date. Marxists haven't much time for it; they regard it as petit bourgeois and not scientific socialism.'

But Forrest displayed no desire to listen to a disquisition on the various kinds of his new faith: he was satisfied with what he had learned from Shaw and had no anxiety to hear any more about socialism, at least not for the time being. But I was not finished with him yet. My new convert had to prove his seriousness by promising to cast his vote for Labour in the coming election.

'But I've never voted in my life!' he objected.

'Then isn't it time you did?'

Forrest admitted that it *was* time and I felt that I had won a recruit to the cause of the contemporary liberal and progressive movement in literature. I even began to imagine how the change in Forrest's social outlook might manifest itself in his next book. It had seemed to me extraordinary – almost incredible – that such a highly cultured writer should have been able to remain so out of touch with the great events of his time – the First World War, the 1916 rebellion in Ireland, the Russian Revolution, the partition of Ireland, the rise of fascism, the Spanish war, the Second World War – and take a conscious decision to ignore them. The truth was that he lived in an imaginative world of his own, the world of childhood and adolescence. The adult world of great poverty and extreme wealth, of deprivation, exploitation and war might not have existed for all he seemed to care about it. The bigotry and violence endemic in Belfast, the city where he had spent the whole of his life, never seemed to impinge on his consciousness. I found all this escapism hard to understand and could not possibly be sympathetic to it. Yet Forrest's middle-class childhood, like my own working-class youth, had been far from idyllic: indeed a reading of *Apostate*, the first part of his autobiography, poignantly reveals how lacking in love his home had been, except of course the love he had given and received from Emma Clery, his nurse. Emotionally, he had been a neglected child, the last of a large family, a child who had found solace in books for the *ennui* of his home in the university area of Belfast. He rebelled against his domestic environment, but only to the extent of rejecting the Christianity of his parents, replacing it with the pantheism he retained for the rest of his life. Socrates was his ideal man, the ancient Greeks his ideal people; judged by this idealistic vision, the spiritual and materialistic atmosphere of twentieth-century Belfast could hardly seem other than charmless at best.

Why then did Forrest choose to live in Belfast? I thought he might find this question difficult to answer, but his answer came swift and direct:

'Because my friends are here.' He looked at me as if to say, 'Could you think of any better reason?' Certainly he had a gift for friendship: despite his physical plainness – even ugliness, of the

67

sort that Socrates himself possessed – Forrest had such an engaging personality and such a variety of interests that I found it impossible to imagine anyone being bored in his company. He talked exceptionally well about the writers he admired: Henry James, Thomas Hardy, Anatole France, Jane Austen, Emily Brontë, Joseph Conrad, Turgenev, Mark Twain and others; he had met and become friends with A.E. and Padraic Colum in Ireland, and Walter de la Mare and E.M. Forster in England; he had corresponded with François Mauriac and James Joyce; he loved music, opera in particular; he had tramped the picture galleries of Italy; and though he was no great traveller he could talk well about London or Bruges or Florence. I should have been satisfied with such a companion and flattered to have gained his friendship, but the truth was that a close friendship between us was impossible. He was old and I was young; he was a bachelor and I was married; he was middle class and genteel and I was working class and not averse to occasional bad language. He once confessed to me that he would not care for the company of a young woman who admitted to having read James Joyce's *Ulysses*: the uninhibited language so disgusted him that he was unable to finish the book. He was not at all pleased when I told him that it was one of my favourite novels and that I had given it to my wife to read before our marriage.

'And what did she think of it?'

'I think she found it difficult.'

'I'm not surprised. It's unreadable!'

'That is what Nora Joyce thought. It *is* boring in places.'

'Unreadable!' Forrest insisted.

How could I agree when I cherished the copy I had bought in Paris in Sylvia Beach's little bookshop on the Left Bank? Forrest's detestation of Joyce's masterpiece, his lack of interest in D.H. Lawrence (I never dared to mention even *Sons and Lovers* in his

68

presence) and his dislike of T.S. Eliot's poetry, all these judgements appeared to me so perverse that my respect for his powers of discrimination began to wither. When he asked me one evening, 'Why do you consider *A Portrait of the Artist as a Young Man* better than my own *Peter Waring*?' I was stumped for a reply; though I admired *Peter Waring* more than any other of his novels, I was convinced that Joyce's novel was incomparably superior. When on another evening he suddenly said to me after a silence in one of our discussions, 'I don't think you really understand me', he spoke the words with such conviction that contradiction was out of the question. For I did not understand him *au fond*. I could not. And the reason was that I never suspected his homosexuality (just as I never suspected E.M. Forster's), though the evidence was all too clear throughout his work.

But it was not clear, at least to me. Homosexuality was then almost a forbidden subject: certainly not one to be lightly introduced into normal conversation. I was aware of Oscar Wilde's life and fate, had read André Gide's *Si le grain ne meurt*, and always associated homosexuality with dandyism. Now, though Forrest's nature and character puzzled me, he could hardly be thought of as a dandy, for he took little interest in his dress or general appearance; nor had he any effeminate traits that might give clues to his real nature. His interest in small boys should have suggested pederasty to me, but whether he ever practised it I have no means of knowing. All I know for certain is that, according to his own account in the opening chapter of *Private Road*, he suffered from 'some mysterious form of arrested development'.

This emotional arrested development may have accounted – at least partly – for his almost total ignorance of politics. But my pleasure when Forrest read *The Intelligent Woman's Guide to Socialism* and declared himself converted to socialism was dissipated the day after the local election. Being eager to hear of his experience at the polling station I called on him at my usual time.

'Well, did you enjoy voting?'

He dropped his head and assumed the look of a small boy who has committed truancy and is ashamed of himself; but the appearance of shame was only play-acting, and not very skilful play-acting at that. Obviously he was amused at something. 'I've seen Knox since I last saw you.'

'Well?'

'He persuaded me not to vote.'

'Did Knox persuade you you to change your mind?'

'Oh no, nothing like that –'

'Then what did?'

'I told him about reading Shaw's book and that it had converted me.'

'And what did Knox say?'

'He said I was being foolish, that he could point out to me the fallacies in Shaw's argument.'

'And did he?'

'No, he hadn't the time. He was in a hurry. Knox is a busy man.'

I was not in the least interested in Knox's busyness and found it hard not to blurt out my opinion that Knox was a fool. 'So why didn't you vote for the Labour candidate? He failed to get in anyway.' In fact he had almost lost his deposit.

'Knox said that I'd have wasted my time voting for him.' He took a long pause. 'But that isn't the real reason why I didn't vote. You'll be angry,' he said, shamefaced. 'At least I think you will.'

I was puzzled, curious, disappointed.

'We began talking about stamps –' Forrest began. 'Knox told

me he possessed two I badly wanted. He offered them to me ...'
there followed a long pause '... on one condition.'

'And what was that?'

'That I didn't go out and vote for your man. Or if I did go out
I'd have to vote for the Unionist. I told him I couldn't do that! Not
after reading Shaw. So it was a kind of compromise, wasn't it?'

I admitted it was and began to laugh. I believe we never
discussed politics again. As a propagandist I was not as good as
I had imagined.

Forrest was awarded the James Black Tait prize for *Young Tom*,
his final novel, which was published in 1944. He was efferves-
cent with delight, saying gleefully as he rubbed his hands
together in self-congratulation, 'Imagine a story about a very
small boy – and nothing else – winning this prize!'

I thought the occasion called for some kind of celebration, but
what kind of celebration would be appropriate I had no notion.
But inspiration struck when I heard that an English touring
opera company was coming to Belfast for a fortnight. Knowing
Forrest's passion for opera I decided to invite him out for the
evening. We chose Smetana's *The Bartered Bride*, or rather the
choice was forced on us for I was then living in Ballymacash and
came to Belfast only at weekends. I asked Forrest what arrangements I should make for his convenience.

'Oh, well, let's see ... Would you care to call for me at, say,
seven o'clock and we'll take a bus to town and walk across to the
Opera House. Would that suit you?'

It suited me admirably. Our seats were in the stalls, we
had a bottle of Guinness each at the intermission, we took
the bus back to Ormiston Crescent, Forrest thanked me, smiled
and said 'Good night', and that was our celebration. I do not
imagine he particularly enjoyed *The Bartered Bride*: the singing

71

and production must have fallen far below the standard he was used to at Covent Garden: as for my hospitality, it could hardly have been called lavish. I had little money at the time, but the truth is I had no idea of what hospitality was required on such an occasion. All the same, I do not believe Forrest was displeased with the attempt I had made to celebrate his literary achievement.

Stephen Gilbert has told me more than once that Forrest considered himself to be a great writer. This surprised me, for I always thought of him as a cult writer, someone whose work could never achieve wide recognition. When he died in 1947 E.M. Forster wrote this about him:

> He was the most important person in Belfast, and, though it would be too much to say that Belfast knew him not, I have sometimes smiled to think how little that great city, engaged in its own ponderous purposes, dreamed of him or indeed of anything.

Forrest died a few months after I had left teaching for broadcasting. He was seventy-three years old and I was thirty-five. Few people attended his funeral – it was private – and I can recall nothing about it except that we left the funeral parlour in Dublin Road opposite the BBC building and made our way to the cemetery at Dundonald, only a mile or so from his house at Ormiston Crescent. I think there was a brief Church of Ireland service and, if I am right, it was unnecessary and inappropriate. Forrest's own religion had little in common with conventional Christianity.

Our friendship had been a literary one and he taught me a lot, but by the time I met him my tastes had been formed and despite his persuasive argument on many writers, we finally had to agree to differ. I had a higher opinion of Forster's novels than he had, I preferred late Yeats to early Yeats, I admired *Ulysses*, his appreciation of Henry James I thought excessive and I could not share his admiration for de la Mare. He often shook his head and smiled when I declared my literary allegiances as if to say, 'I cannot possibly agree with you, but go on, I'm interested to hear your point of view.'

I remember that when he was admitted to hospital for a while during the last year of his life, he brought with him his French editions of Turgenev and impressed upon me that none of the English translations were good enough. This was not literary snobbery on his part but an example of his discrimination. And of course he was right. I followed his advice. And I gave my friends the same advice – but without acknowledging its source.

5

Broadcasting House in Belfast was a part of the *British* Broadcasting Corporation and the ethos was definitely non-Irish. The emphasis was almost entirely on the 'Ulster' way of life, and 'Ulster' was defined as the Six Counties only, and the Six Counties were predominantly Protestant. The staff in Broadcasting House contained only a few Catholics, of whom none held senior posts, and none were producers. This was no accident but a deliberate policy of exclusion. Catholics were considered to be untrustworthy for posts of responsibility, and many years had to pass before the question of religious discrimination was confronted, as I'm told it now has been.

Despite this religious bias – which was never admitted by the hierarchy on the few occasions the subject was raised in conversation – the BBC in Belfast was a pleasant place of employment. There were only about a dozen producers and we all knew one another well, as we met together every Thursday morning at eleven to discuss our programmes and drink coffee. Harry McMullan, the Head of Programmes, took the chair and skilfully steered the business along with good humour and tact. As a chairman he was at his best. His judgement of programmes seldom coincided with my own and at programme board I had a habit of speaking out bluntly what was in my mind concerning our output. I saw no reason not to call a radio play 'rubbish' when it clearly was rubbish, or not to call a short story 'trivial' when it was trivial. By commenting harshly on my own programmes I felt I had given myself the right to be equally harsh on the output of my colleagues. Tact was certainly not my forte. As I had a taste for controversy I liked to provoke it – especially when programme board assumed the form of a mutual admiration society: which it frequently did.

When I joined the BBC the Station Director (I think that was the proper designation) was George Marshall, a Scot with an unsmiling, granite-like face, who was reputed to spend a good deal of time in the Ulster Reform Club in Castle Place. Marshall retired soon after my arrival and never took any opportunity to speak to me, being content to pass me by in the corridor with a slight nod. Aloofness, apparently, was part of the legacy of the great Lord Reith, another Scot, who had shaped the BBC. But one Lord Reith, in my view, was quite enough. When Marshall retired I was told he spent more and more of his time in his club and that his fellow members took to avoiding him once he had relinquished his reins of office. By the time he died, he was a forgotten figure. His widow, a striking-looking American, with a beautiful complexion even in her eighties, went into business as a hairdresser and long outlived her husband. The Marshall regime was not a glorious one and I cannot recall anyone saying a complimentary word on his behalf until many years later when I met Joyce Cary in Oxford. Over a cup of tea in his front room at Parks Road, Cary, in his brisk, inconsequential manner, suddenly asked me if I knew Marshall. 'I heard he went to seed. Is that true?'

'Yes, I believe so.'

'What a pity! He was a splendid-looking chap when I knew him at Oxford. Very good company and very talented ... You know, he could very well have become a concert pianist. He was a first-class player – or at least he had that potentiality. Poor George! So that's what happened to him.'

I cannot now help contrasting the lives of the two men: one who fulfilled himself, the other who did not. Cary had a rich and varied life as a painter, a civil servant, a soldier, and most notably as a novelist; the death of his wife and one of his sons brought him much sorrow, and finally he had to bear the suffering of a form of sclerosis that left him paralysed. Most of Marshall's life was spent as a BBC administrator in Belfast, and the thought occurred to me more than once that to stay overlong in my native city was to court failure.

Joyce Cary's disease had not yet manifested itself at the period of my visit, and I remember that he expressed the desire to return to Derry and Donegal for a holiday: if he did so we would arrange to meet again. We never did. But my visit to Parks Road was not fruitless: I arranged to have a couple of his stories broadcast, for Cary, having been born in Derry, qualified as an 'Ulster' writer, though as far as I could gather he was imaginatively interested only in Donegal, which lay on the wrong side of the truncated province. Cary exemplified the absurdity of trying to divide writers into categories devised by politicians. And by persuasion and some guile I got the Head of Programmes to accept my point of view. He was not entirely inflexible.

McMullan, who died in 1988, always struck me as a man too often out of his depth to be happy. He had been educated at a public school in the Isle of Man, a reporter in the Unionist *Belfast News-Letter* before drifting into broadcasting, and when he returned from war service in the navy he was put in charge of programmes. It would have been a difficult job for a tough, confident and well-qualified man but McMullan appeared to me fragile both physically and intellectually; he was one of the thinnest men I have ever seen, with a long, pale, lugubrious face and a restless manner. When I had to consult him in his office he was usually smoking a cigarette and at the same time chewing a handkerchief to rags. He lacked confidence in himself and in his producers, and in my view had many of the ingrained prejudices of middle-class Protestants of that time. He was no reader, though he once admitted to having read *The Cruel Sea* and recommended it to me, informing me that it was a best-seller. I have not yet read it.

But he could be witty and charming, and was perhaps tougher than his looks suggested. In many ways I seemed to puzzle him. For instance I dressed badly and never wore a suit unless a formal occasion demanded it; my accent was recognisably 'Belfast' and therefore 'common' and not suitable for broadcast-ing – except as a vehicle for comedy parts. And he could not understand how with my working-class background I had managed to graduate from two universities. I remember his astonishment when he learned that my father had been an engine-driver on the Belfast and County Down Railway.

'But I understand you went to the university.'

'Yes, that's right.'

'How did you manage that?'

'I got scholarships.'

'Oh.'

Harry had gone straight from school into journalism, and like most people who missed university he overvalued the experi-ence. In his view I was something of an oddity, to be watched and not given too much licence. I had felt unsure of myself during my first couple of years in the BBC, but after five or six years I think I must have overcompensated and my former diffidence turned into arrogance. At morning coffee in the canteen I made no effort to hide my opinions and made it known that I was a socialist who held no religious beliefs. This might well have been common-place in sophisticated London, but in Northern Ireland, the most remote of the regions, such views were regarded as heretical, beyond the pale.

But I worked hard, being sometimes responsible for seven programmes in a week (which meant that my secretary was also overworked) and our efforts were rewarded by what were called Merit Awards – annual sums of money, which came in very handy.

After a year or so Elizabeth and I were able to save enough money to put down a deposit for a small semi-detached house in an estate overlooking Belfast Lough. This estate was one of the cheapest in the city, built with the aid of a government subsidy and, as we soon discovered, jerry-built and uncomfortable. I seemed to be unlucky in finding a reasonably good house, but I suppose we were lucky to have any kind of house at all. But we did not take this unfortunate bad buy from a speculative builder without protest, and I helped to organise a residents' committee (and found myself elected chairman) in order to fight a legal case against the speculator and the Stormont ministry which had backed his enterprise. Half a dozen activists carried on the campaign for redress, holding committee meetings, consulting lawyers and badgering the responsible civil servants. The final result was neither victory nor defeat but the almost inevitable compromise of being allowed to resell our houses but at a price much less than that we had paid for them. After much discussion some of us, including most of our committee, accepted the offer and cleared out, disgruntled that our fellow residents had been so apathetic throughout the fight. I concluded from this experi-ence that the lower middle class made dubious allies in any struggle for a good cause, having no sense of solidarity and little stomach for a fight against the pillars of society. Obviously Ibsen's great realist dramas of nineteenth-century Norway still had relevance – and particularly to Ireland.

Although not combative by temperament – indeed I was all for a quiet life with a book somewhere near at hand – I somehow found myself getting into scrapes, especially with those in authority above me. The constraints I encountered in the world of broadcasting – censorship of scripts and avoidance of certain subjects as being too controversial – I thought not only irrational but laughable. I was not foolish enough to deny that too much freedom could prove to be almost as bad as too little, but I was all for taking risks in the hope that they would work out and not bring some kind of disaster in their train. Probably I had an anarchistic streak in my own nature; I suspect everybody has and that it sometimes has to be curbed; but to quench it, or allow it to be quenched, seemed to me a diminution and a distortion of the human spirit.

Our next move was to a Victorian terraced house in Dunluce Avenue, a legacy from one of Elizabeth's uncles, an old, eccentric bearded farmer who lived alone near Ballygowan in a small and neglected farmhouse. Sam, whose appearance suggested an Old Testament patriarch, or one of the biblical figures in Blake's paintings, seldom spoke, ate little, slept in rags, and lived the life of a hermit, hardly venturing beyond the three or four fields he owned and rented out to neighbours. He had a gentle, un-worldly disposition and probably never hurt a fly in his life; he spent his days wandering about the fields, fetching water from the well, eating his frugal meals, and reading the great family Bible in the evenings until darkness fell. In winter he seldom bothered to light his oil lamp, preferring to sit by the fireside during the hours of darkness before retiring to his cold, unaired bed. He was, I suppose, an extreme example of Protestant puritanism and what the purpose of his life was I can only guess at. Whatever it may have been we could count ourselves as the beneficiaries of his self-neglect.

The Dunluce Avenue house, with its three bedrooms and two attics, suited us because it was only a quarter of an hour's walk from the BBC and a couple of minutes' walk from Methodist College, the school where Deirdre, our daughter, and Brian and Gavin, our two sons, were sent. It was also near Queen's University, whose library I used – much more now than when I was an undergraduate or when I was engaged in postgraduate research. The library had undergone a change since the thirties when almost the whole of twentieth-century literature was missing from its shelves. The library assistant, I discovered, was now an almost unknown poet from the Midlands of England called Philip Larkin, tall, thin and shy, with a slight stammer, whom I persuaded to broadcast, explaining to him that I would edit out his speech defect if that proved to be necessary. I think this was the first occasion on which Larkin ever broadcast. Even when his poetry became famous he showed little inclination to read his work on radio or to appear on television.

I may be giving the impression that literary programmes were my main output. This was not so. They were the programmes that gave me the most pleasure to originate and produce. But current affairs also interested me greatly. When I began at the BBC these talks were the monopoly of John E. Sayers, who became the editor of the *Belfast Telegraph*, by far the most widely read newspaper in Northern Ireland.

Sayers and I were about the same age and I was responsible for his regular fifteen-minute programmes called 'Ulster Commentary'. He had pale regular features, was always dressed neatly, and had adopted the habit of strolling along the street as if to suggest he was a man of leisure rather than a busy journalist. He had a slightly high-pitched voice and spoke with a pronounced English accent that I thought affected. Like his friend Harry McMullan, he had served in the British Navy during the Second World War; both men – to my mind – possessed dull middle-class Protestant characteristics which I found unsympathetic. They were middle-aged and middlebrow and politically middle of the road, a combination of attributes that I translated for myself as stuffy, bland, and uninspiring: in short, they were conformists. Yet my working relationship with Sayers was harmonious, because I found him pleasant and thoughtful, and lacking the pomposity his manner might have suggested. The problem was that I contested McMullan's judgement that the commentaries were objective commentaries on the Ulster political scene. Indeed I considered them as merely extended first leaders of the *Belfast Telegraph*, with all that implied of diluted unionism. Sayers unquestionably was a competent journalist and broadcaster and his commentaries were a valuable contribution to regional radio, but I argued that speakers with different political views should be invited to substitute for him, and after a long delay my arguments prevailed. So I invited J.J. Campbell, a nationalist and liberal-minded Catholic and J.U. Stewart, an equally liberal-minded Protestant and a Labour Party supporter to broadcast commentaries in counterbalance to Sayers. He, with his usual graciousness, told me he approved of the change, confessing that he found the chore of writing scripts more and more of a strain. Sometimes he appeared in the studio looking very tired and I was aware that he suffered from high blood pressure.

I am glad that, a few years before his death, Sayers was given an honorary doctorate at Queen's for his services to journalism.

I think J.J. Campbell, who was a member of the senate of the university, recommended Sayers for this honour. Certainly the two became friends and always spoke warmly of each other, despite their diametrically opposed politics. Campbell was slightly older than Sayers, dark-haired and handsome, with a ready smile and wit; a classical scholar, he once told me he had been a hairdresser and had to work his way through Queen's. I found J.J. very good company, and Jim Stewart too, though a lot of people thought Jim too blunt in manner and too outspoken in his opinions to be happy in his company. I enjoyed his bluntness and outspokenness and as I shared most of his political views we got on well together, so well that I often called at his house when I felt in need of stimulating talk: mostly economics (which he taught in the College of Technology), politics, both local and international (which he loved to discuss) and not least gossip (for he took pleasure in pointing out the frailties of our friends). We agreed that chat without malice was like chips without fish. His wife Sophie, a Canadian painter, was an attentive listener, only occasionally interrupting to ejaculate, 'Oh, Jim, what a thing to say about a friend!' He would usually counter with, 'Is it true what I'm sayin' or isn't it? Come on, out wi' the truth!' Jim's father had been the caretaker of May Street Presbyterian church, a church renowned for one of its ministers called Wylie Blue, whose oratory had attracted even an unbeliever like myself, but only because his style was so histrionic as to be ham. Jim Stewart profoundly distrusted orators of any kind, particularly clerics, and expounded his own ideas in a dry caustic tone; he scorned the pseudo-anglified accent of the Belfast middle class, and made no attempt to pronounce his final g's. Like Campbell, Stewart had obtained a degree by his own initiative and would proudly declare that he had spent his teens working in the shipyard while people like myself were still attending school to get the social polish he thought so useful for entry to a university. When Jim became a part-time university lecturer himself, he would boast – justifiably – of his achievement. He was a pungent broadcaster whose natural style made a refreshing contrast to the 'naiceness' of so many others. I can recall his being banned for a while for alleged 'irresponsibility' when in a discussion programme he accused charities (without naming them) of spending a disproportionate amount of the money donated by the public on well-paid salaries for their full-time officials. Whether Stewart could have substantiated his allegation – he told me he could – I have no means of knowing; all I do know is that his broadcasting was terminated for at least a year. I was not a party to the consultations, such decisions being the prerogative of senior management. In the BBC's carefully graded hierarchical structure, a producer quickly became aware of his position as halfway up and halfway down. At times he was made to feel important, at other times a cog in a complicated machine whose internal workings were none of his business. I have used the word 'he' for convenience and because very few women were appointed to be producers in the period immediately after the Second World War.

I have mentioned Campbell, Sayers and Stewart because each was important in his own way in the Belfast of forty years ago and all are now almost forgotten. Sayers tried to liberalise the Unionist Party and had a little success, but not enough; it came too late and he died too early, perhaps a martyr to political intransigence. He certainly died a disappointed man. Campbell, with his classical education, his greater sense of political realism and, above all, his sense of humour, was better equipped than Sayers to face the harsh facts of public life. His expectation of social *rapprochement* between the Catholic minority and the Protestant majority was governed by his sense of history (again something which Sayers lacked), and in the last years of his life when he became a Professor of Education at Queen's he appeared to have found a niche he liked. Stewart, too, possessed a happy (even a happy-go-lucky) strain in his nature, which appeared when Sophie and he gave New Year's parties for their friends; on these occasions Jim always looked remarkably youthful, despite his almost entire baldness, and displayed his finesse as a dancer – which gave his women friends much pleasure. He died suddenly of a heart attack while in the lavatory; maybe it was not a dignified death but it was a swift one, and one he would not have minded. Jim never put any stress on dignity during his lifetime and the manner of his death would have appealed to his wry sense of humour. I missed his friendship, especially after I got to know him well during a holiday we spent in the USSR. He insisted on taking me to a football match during our stay in Moscow, but it turned out to be a rough game with three or four players being sent off. I became more interested in a young man who sat next to me, a Moscovite, who during the course of the game was absorbed in trying to work out mathematical problems, and only occasionally looked up from his notebook to follow an exciting moment of play. Jim, a fervent supporter of a now defunct Irish League team called Distillery, growled at me, 'I thought we'd have seen a better match than this. My team would've beaten either of them easily.'

Queen's University and the BBC were, I suppose, the two most prominent cultural centres in Belfast, but whether either was completely conscious of its role is a matter of doubt. The university produced a steady stream of doctors, dentists, scientists, engineers and so on, but the arts faculty was small and some of its professors were not of the first rank. The more lively students referred to the university as an overgrown technical college, and either graduated as quickly as possible or fell by the

84

wayside and left. Even though my own experience had not been a happy one, and I had left with relief, when I joined the BBC I was determined that some kind of alliance should take place between the two institutions. Only one academic – Estyn Evans – seemed to have realised the potential of broadcasting. The English department seemed to be living in a different century. Professor F.W. Baxter frequented the library and was often seen with a bundle of books in his arms, so he must have read a great deal. But he published nothing, lectured poorly and was cursed with a New Zealand accent that made his reading of poetry memorable for its lack of euphony. I ruled him out as a possibility. A newcomer, J.I.M. Stewart, who wrote detective stories under the name of Michael Innes, arrived at Queen's and proved to be an excellent broadcaster. Unfortunately his stay in Belfast was brief, else he would have been an acquisition. Many years later, when he wrote his autobiography he confessed to finding Queen's 'drowsy' and his professor 'a dormouse', which was more or less my own conclusion.

Still, I was determined that the university should somehow be brought within the orbit of broadcasting. There appeared to be prejudices on both sides. Some academics sniffed at the notion of 'popularisation': they considered their disciplines too precious and esoteric for such an activity. As for our local BBC, nobody seemed to think that professors had any popular wares to sell. But when Eric Ashby was appointed vice-chancellor he at once accepted an invitation to broadcast and to bring 'town' and 'gown' together and only laughed when I told him of the prejudices. 'All that will have to be changed.' It was. The alliance was made and Ashby's lead was soon followed. Academics are supposed to be independently minded, but I sometimes wonder.

The hours I worked as a radio producer continued to be so long and irregular that I spent little time at home during the week and really only saw Elizabeth and our three children at weekends. The conditions of employment were serf-like. To quote the contract I signed in 1946:

> Paragraph two. You agree to devote the whole of your time and attention to the service of the Corporation and to attend for duty at such hours of the day or night as shall from time to time be decided by the Corporation.

Other paragraphs followed about not writing or engaging in public speaking. I had no desire to practise public speaking but every desire to go on trying to write, though I was very confused about the literary form that would best suit my talent – that is, assuming I had any. Of course I tried to persuade myself that I had. But what had I done? Nothing, except a few short stories and essays, plus a couple of attempts at writing a novel. Altogether, nothing much to boast about. Yet Forrest Reid had encouraged me; Austin Clarke, reviewing an anthology called *Northern Harvest* in the *Irish Times* had picked out for comment my short story called 'Before Marriage'; Seumas O'Sullivan had published a couple of my essays in his *Dublin Magazine*; Oliver Edwards, a fine German scholar who had been acquainted with Yeats, had praised a lyric that had appeared in the *Irish Times*; and a poem I had written as an exercise one afternoon in Murlough Bay had appeared in a Faber anthology of Irish poetry edited by Robert Greacen and Valentin Iremonger. But what were these but bits and pieces by a budding author who had taken far too much time budding and looked like continuing to bud *ad infinitum*. As an editor of *Lagan* I had of course got to know a lot of writers and enjoyed working with them. And now, as a radio producer, it looked as if my fate was to be merely a friend of writers and not a writer myself. The BBC had bought my services for the sum of £690 a year and I had to keep my mouth shut in public and forgo all ambition to write what it pleased me to write. The complication was that I loved my radio work, I loved working with words, I loved the excitement of a broadcasting studio, and I saw no possibility of changing my way of life.

My workload was lightened eventually, after I had been four or five years with the BBC, when a second talks producer was appointed to look after farming and gardening. My colleague was Brian Branston, a cheerful and energetic Yorkshireman a few years younger than I, who impressed me by his strong sense of independence, his intelligence and his ability to master a subject quickly. He arrived in Belfast with an old Rover car – which we later shared, following one of Brian's periodical financial crises – a wife whom he had recently acquired, along with a small family which was soon increased, and an air of high spirits that suggested an irreverence towards authority untypical of the kind of Englishman that usually gravitated to Northern Ireland.

We got on extremely well together and instead of discussing ideas for programmes in our office we would occasionally take the Rover to Helen's Bay and walk along the shore. There, by the sea, we would chat about literature – Brian had a first-class honours degree in English – or about politics or about personal affairs. I remember a long talk about methods of birth control during which I told him about the monthly rhythm method, which he promised to try. He did, but without success. Or rather with unexpected success, for after a few months his wife became pregnant again. I think he was pleased, though he swore he would never trust my mathematics again.

Brian proved to be too lively a character to remain in this post for long. He had a row over some misdemeanour he had committed – something to do with having inadvertently advertised a farming product – and he promptly left. He found a similar post in the radio talks department in London and later transferred to television. During his short stay in Belfast he wrote an authoritative book on farming that was published by Faber, though on his arrival here he had denied all knowledge of the subject. I believe he also found time to translate *Beowulf*, the great Anglo-Saxon epic, and to attempt a novel set in Iceland, a country he had never visited. As Icelandic sagas fascinated him, he was confident that he could write a new one. The paragraph in the BBC contract about giving the whole of his time to the Corporation he treated as a joke. I should have followed his example of insubordination.

Brian Branston was the kind of colleague I liked to have: not a Corporation man first and last, but very much his own man, serving the BBC well but without sacrificing his own individuality; he was the opposite of a yes-man. Sam Hanna Bell had the same qualities. He had an erratic streak that sometimes surfaced unexpectedly, when he would seek company to break the loneliness of writing his scripts. He would come into my office and suggest going across the road to the Elbow Room for a drink. This pub, only a hundred yards away, had a friendly, slightly sleazy atmosphere downstairs; there was a long stained table on one side of the bar, opposite the smelly gents lavatory with its small broken window, which overlooked the subterranean Blackstaff river. On the other side of the bar were enclosed snugs, each able to hold about half a dozen customers, three on either side, knee to knee, with a door for privacy.

I remember one afternoon when Sam and I escaped from our offices to this relaxing sanctuary and we were joined by Jack Loudan, a sandy-haired ex-journalist who was then in charge of CEMA – the Council for the Encouragement of Music and the Arts, the organisation which preceded the Northern Ireland

Arts Council. Jack was a good conversationalist, a playwright and the author of a book on Amanda McKittrick Ros, the novelist from Larne whose euphuistic style had attracted the attention of Aldous Huxley and Denis Johnston. Sam was himself an engaging conversationalist and the hours passed quickly until Jack, pointing to a travelling bag at his feet, announced that he was bound for London that evening and wanted to be on board the Heysham boat well before sailing time; he asked us to go with him by taxi to the docks, and join him on board the boat for a final drink to round off the evening. I decided not to go, but Sam accepted Jack's invitation. The next morning I got a telephone call from Sam.

'I'm ringing from Manchester ...'

'From where?'

'Manchester. From the BBC here ...'

'Oh ... Anything wrong?'

'No, all's well ... I want you to do something for me if you're not too busy at the moment ...'

On Sam's return he told me what had happened. The conversation in the ship's bar had become more and more engrossing and when Sam asked the steward whether the time hadn't arrived for him to leave, the steward had replied, 'Sir, you cannot disembark now. We are already past the Isle of Man.' When Sam enquired what had happened to me I told him that I had taken a walk home by the most circuitous route I could think of, and arrived home at midnight exhausted but sober.

I frequented the Elbow Room – now long demolished – a good deal and do not regret the time spent or misspent in the snugs of that friendly pub. It was one of the hazards of the job to drink there after a broadcast. Captain R.H. Davis, a gruff old seafarer, always insisted that we should fortify ourselves with tots of rum, one before and one after each of his fifteen-minute broadcasts describing the adventures he had had on sailing ships. Though no Conrad – indeed his style and delivery were monotonous – he was a popular broadcaster and an agreeable drinking companion. His scripts had one great merit: what he said about his voyages rang true. And that was enough for our listeners, if not for me, for I had more mandarinic notions of 'style' then than I have now.

The Elbow Room was a gathering place for BBC staff who liked its relaxed atmosphere, which was such a relief from the stratified atmosphere of Broadcasting House where people moved along the corridors a little too conscious of their status and responsibilities: a nervous announcer mouthing a page of late news and hurrying to his small studio; a flurried secretary on the heels of her producer; an engineer poring over a technical manual; a commissionaire in a nondescript uniform directing people to studios and offices, with a message boy to guide them. Broadcasting House was all busyness: the Elbow Room – known as Studio E – was all relaxation. There, time came to a stop.

The BBC seemed to attract dissatisfied teachers and clergymen. W.R. Rodgers, always referred to as Bertie, was a Presbyterian clergyman who appeared to be settled for life in the small church of Cloveneden in the heart of County Armagh; his wife Marie was a doctor, and two children were born of the union; life might have been idyllic for such a couple, one caring for the spiritual needs of the little community, the other for the physical. But things fell apart. Bertie and Marie each had too many contrarieties and tensions to lead a quiet life. Bertie gained a reputation for his poetry with the publication in 1941 of his first volume *Awake and Other Poems*; Marie became mentally ill; misunderstandings and quarrels became frequent and sometimes violent. Their pastoral life in Armagh came to an end.

I already knew the background of Rodgers's life before he joined the BBC in 1946, for I had first encountered him before the war, and already we had met several times in John Hewitt's flat in Mount Charles. As a poet-clergyman who contributed to the *New Statesman* and could be met in pubs without his dog collar, Bertie was a unique figure in Belfast and naturally the subject of gossip. He had been brought up in The Mount, a middle-class enclave a couple of hundred yards from Chatsworth Street where I had spent my early childhood. On Sunday mornings I used to take a walk up The Mount not only to admire the big houses there but also to stand at the Mountpottinger corner to enjoy the Salvation Army band perform for half an hour before they marched down the road to their Citadel at the top of Carleton Street where my maternal grandparents lived. My slow, circuitous walk would have pleased Bertie if I had ever told him about it, but I never did. For he himself had the habit of approaching people and topics slowly and circuitously, believing this method was best to get to the heart of a man or a subject.

I do not think Bertie made friends quickly; certainly three or four years passed before I got to know him at all intimately. It was the same with Louis MacNeice, who liked to look and listen long before accepting you as a friend. In the BBC in London, Bertie and Louis were always coupled together because both were in the features department (under Laurence Gilliam, a man with the gift of leadership), both were Irishmen from Belfast, both were poets, and both were heavy drinkers who seemed to spend more time in pubs than in studios or their offices. Altogether both were unconventional and elusive characters.

I never saw Bertie conduct a church service, but I once saw him mount a pulpit and deliver a short sermon to a congregation of one – myself. I cannot recall anything of what he said but he looked impressive standing slightly sideways as his usually soft voice resonated in the empty church. He loved words, perhaps he loved them too well; he was by nature a taciturn and diffident man who, when he was sober, used words sparingly, but when drunk he would scatter them so extravagantly that his hearers could hardly believe their ears.

When he climbed the pulpit of the beautiful eighteenth-century Presbyterian church in Randalstown which he had insisted that we visit, Bertie looked to me what at heart he was, a clergyman whose vocation gave him an enormous sense of purpose. His pale face, with its large limpid dark-brown eyes, full lips and downturned mouth, seemed to emanate calm and rest. It was the face of a man in the middle of life and at peace with himself. Yet I knew he was not at peace either with himself or with his world. To my eyes he always looked ill at ease when we met in London, and we always made our way to a pub or a club – the George or the Mandrake – to while away the afternoon gossiping about Ireland and our friends: John Hewitt, Sam Bell, George and Mercy MacCann in Belfast, Frank O'Connor, Sean O'Faolain and Ben Kiely in Dublin. And there was always an enquiry about Michael J. Murphy in south Armagh, whom we both thought a saintlike man dedicated to his lifetime's task of gathering folklore.

That Rodgers was a tortured and guilt-ridden man for most of his adult life can hardly be doubted by anyone who knew him. But he never – at least to me – voiced what his tortures and guilts were. In 1953 I was working for a while in London, and one afternoon was standing in the foyer of Broadcasting House, a little too early for an appointment, when I saw Bertie running out of the lift, his light overcoat trailing the ground.

'Hello, Bertie!' I called, going forward to greet him.

'Marie has killed herself.'

He ran on, his face stricken. I learned later in the day that he had just heard this news before he had spoken to me and was already on his way back to Ireland. It was the only occasion on which I saw him out of control, a ghostly figure in flight. I had never met Marie, and Bertie never talked to me about his private life. Soon afterwards I did meet Marianne Helweg, the former wife of Laurence Gilliam, whom Bertie later married. I had, of course, heard the gossip about their relationship but took little interest in it. The puritanism of Lord Reith's day had long disappeared from the BBC, but Bertie's position in the features department, with Gilliam as his boss, was still an awkward one, to say the least. One day when MacNeice was in Belfast, he brought up the subject as we were walking along the Dublin Road towards Shaftsbury Square on our way to the MacCanns' flat.

'I want to ask your advice,' he said suddenly, in his harsh nasal voice.

'Yes?'

'About Bertie. You know how he's fixed ... '

'Yes. He's married Marianne.'

'That makes everything very difficult.'

'I suppose so.'

'Anyhow, I should like to have your opinion,' Louis continued, taking his long loping strides, which I found hard to keep up with. 'He asked me what he should do. Should he resign from the BBC? I told him yes. Was I right, d'you think?'

I didn't answer him at once, as he appeared to value what I thought about the matter. 'No. I think you were wrong.'

'You mean, I gave him bad advice?'

'I think so.'

Louis was taken aback because normally I deferred to him unless we were talking about rugby football; then, after George MacCann told him that I had played a couple of seasons with Instonians, he always deferred to me.

'Why d'you think I was wrong?'

I gave him my reasons: if Bertie resigned from the BBC he might have difficulty in finding another job; he had left the Church and might not be welcomed back even if he wanted to go back; though he had a degree he was now middle-aged and had no experience of teaching, so that avenue might be closed to him too; and he certainly was not the journalistic type. Louis remained silent, brooding over my arguments for Bertie's unemployability.

'What about you people in Belfast?' he asked.

'No, I don't think so.'

'Why not?'

'Because of his reputation.'

'You don't think he would fit in?'

'He might or he mightn't. *They* would think not.'

'But couldn't you drop a word in the right ears?'

I said I could, and I did; but it was to no avail. My suggestion that Rodgers would be an acquisition to the local staff was received coolly, as I had expected it would be, but at least I had made soundings. When a vacancy turned up for an extra features producer Bertie got in touch with me and asked what his chances would be. I told him that I did not know (though I did) and advised him to apply. I never learned whether he did or not, and I never asked him. A young inexperienced man, a teacher, got the job. Bertie was driven to take a post in an advertising agency, though later he returned to the BBC as a freelance writer; but neither advertising nor freelance work suited him and he was often short of money.

One morning at half past nine my secretary, Frances Jackson, arrived in my office and found Bertie asleep in the big armchair, looking completely exhausted. He had come off the Stranraer–Larne ferry. She worked quietly at her desk until I appeared about an hour later, whereupon she shushed me with her finger to her mouth and pointed to Bertie still asleep. He awoke shortly afterwards, and Frances – always a ministering angel – brought him black coffee and a bun. Then he told me his tale, Frances having discreetly retired from the office. He had left London after a day's drinking, had continued drinking on the train to Stranraer, and then on the boat to Larne. He had had nothing to eat for two days. He had come across to clear up some domestic matters, was broke and tired and shyly asked me could I help him.

I had only a couple of pounds in my pocket, not enough for his urgent needs. He needed about £15 and the only way I could think of to find this sum quickly was to commission him to write immediately a 2,000-word talk on any topic he chose; I would arrange to have it recorded in the afternoon (if a studio and a recording engineer could be made available) and Frances would seek the co-operation of Miss Maureen Moore, the Programme Executive, who had the authority to make out a cheque for the proposed programme. Miss Moore, who was well acquainted with the vagaries of producers, gave her agreement: a cheque would be ready for Mr Rodgers as soon as the recording had been made. A studio would be vacant at three o'clock for rehearsal and the recording would be made at four. So all was well: the engineers and the bureaucracy were prepared to spring into action. The only remaining problem was Bertie. Would he – or could he – write 2,000 words in a couple of hours? He shook his head sadly, but I refused to accept his negative.

'I've never done anything like this before,' he said, looking at me with his great brown eyes, like a schoolboy facing a bully of a schoolmaster who had set an unreasonable task. 'Impossible,' he repeated. 'I'd like to do it if I could. It would solve everything, wouldn't it?'

It was my turn to nod sadly.

Bertie paused for a long while. 'I know, I know, I know,' he said, almost to himself. 'It's very good of you and I'm grateful. But I've nothing to write about. There's nothing in my mind, so how could I do what you ask?'

I suggested he might write about his life in London, especially angled on Ulster people there whom he knew and who were prominent in theatrical and literary circles. It was by no means a brilliant suggestion and the only person I remember mentioning was Joe Tomelty who at that time had a leading role in a West End play. Bertie agreed to make an attempt and we brought him to the Board Room where he would not be interrupted. Two hours of anguish followed, with cups of coffee and sandwiches and dictation to my secretary, who rapidly prepared a typescript. When I told Bertie that he had performed as fast as Trollope – about 250 words every quarter of an hour – he gave a wry smile. He had the reputation of being a tortoise of a writer, and some of his poems had taken years to complete. That I knew, just as I knew that the polished and punning sentences of his prose were fashioned slowly and carefully, indeed wrought much too carefully for my taste.

W.R. Rodgers was a fine poet, highly praised in his lifetime, and now, a couple of decades after his death, almost forgotten. But some day the pendulum will swing in his favour. Take for instance his sensual lyric 'The Net' with its imperative beginning and end:

Quick, woman, in your net
Catch the silver I fling!
O I am deep in your debt,
Draw tight, skin-tight, the string,
And rake the silver in.

No fisher ever yet
Drew such a cunning ring ...

Come, make no sound, my sweet;
Turn down the candid lamp
And draw the equal quilt
Over our naked guilt.

I cannot say that the talk cobbled together that day turned out
to be memorable – indeed it was a scrappy effort that he must
have been ashamed of. When the recording was over we hurried
out of the building and across the road to the Elbow Room where
Bertie – an infrequent but well-recognised customer – had his
cheque cashed. With money in his pocket and after a drink or
two, his equanimity returned and we both relaxed. On this
occasion our stay in the pub was short: Bertie had urgent
domestic business to attend to; but the financial crisis was over,
at least for the time being. There were many crises in Bertie's life,
and he could have done with fewer. I remember one thing he
said just before we parted on that occasion. 'Well, I've met my
two worst enemies today and had a victory over both.' He was
referring to the microphone in the BBC studio that we had left
and the glass of whiskey that he had just drunk.

Rodgers and MacNeice burnt themselves out prematurely;
neither lived long enough to collect a pension. Louis struck me
as being the tougher man, with his long, dark, toothy Irish face,
his tall, slightly awkward figure, and his ability to dismiss with
a frowning stare anyone whose company he found disagreeable.
I was not surprised to learn that as a schoolboy he had been a
robust but not very skilful rugby forward and, of course, his
interest in the game was lifelong. When Ireland was playing in
Dublin, he usually contrived to see the match. On one occasion,
a couple of days before an international, he telephoned me to tell

me that he wanted to meet a writer called Tom Skelton who lived near Carrickfergus and asked if was there any chance of my being free so that we could go together; we might also go to Dublin together. I *was* free and we went in my car to Carrickfergus – Louis depended on his friends for favours and of course reciprocated – but unfortunately when we called at Skelton's bungalow he was not at home. I do not think Louis had written to warn him of his visit. Anyway he was not in the least upset by this contretemps.

'Would you like to see my father's church?'

'I would.'

'Pity Skelton wasn't in. Sorry to have missed him. Next time better luck maybe.'

I do not think there was a next time; at any rate MacNeice never produced a feature written by Tom Skelton. This was certainly a pity, for it might have advanced Skelton's career. He had written an interesting book called *Clay Under Clover*, which had been published by Gollancz, and was contributing articles to the *Manchester Guardian* and talks to the BBC in Belfast. But after this promising start his career seemed to falter and I have sometimes wondered what happened to him. Louis certainly took no further interest in Skelton's career; he was more concerned to visit his father's church, which we walked round in silence.

> I was the rector's son, born to the anglican order,
>> Banned for ever from the candles of the Irish poor;
> The Chichesters knelt in marble at the end of a transept
>> With ruffs about their necks, their portion sure.

This was the first time I felt that Louis had a profound love of Ireland, that his enthusiastic support of the Irish rugby team was a genuine feeling and not a sentimental adolescent pose. I should, of course, have known better, for his love of Ireland appears in many poems and in his study of W.B. Yeats. Certainly he was devoted to his father.

How Louis wrote so much, read so much, travelled so much, drank so much and had so much time for his friends baffled me. Once we were walking in Belfast past the old Group Theatre when he stopped suddenly and addressed me seriously.

'Are you a drinking man?'

'No, I wouldn't call myself one. I drink irregularly but seldom seriously.'

'I drink *very* regularly and *very* seriously.'

This was at the time his play *Traitors in Our Way* was being produced at the Group. He looked up at the playbill and I thought he was about to ask me what I thought of his play and was glad he did not. For I had disliked it. Perhaps it is a much better play than I thought, but when I saw it on the opening night I found it unconvincing and smart, a piece in the style of Somerset Maugham, something aimed at the West End, but given a provincial rep production. I had been bored and embarrassed – and distressed for Louis's sake. After the performance a few of his friends joined him in the BBC club. He was in serious drinking form but after midnight he broke away from the bar and challenged me to a game of table tennis. I was not a good player but I was too good for Louis when he was sober and much too good for him when he was drunk. When I let him win some games he soon noticed I was doing so deliberately.

'You're not trying now!' he shouted across the table.

'I am,' I lied.

But he knew I was not, and threw down his bat in disgust and returned to the bar.

Sometimes, when drunk, Louis became lecherous; but the women he singled out for attention usually were flattered by his overtures. Though he spent a great deal of his time in pubs with men, he also relished the company of women and patently attracted their admiration. Rodgers, on the other hand, when drinking deep, seemed to drift away from the company he was in and commune with himself, sometimes silently, sometimes in a whirlpool of words that appeared to put him into a kind of trance.

I never discussed their poetry with either Rodgers or MacNeice – it seemed too intimate a matter for chat. But MacNeice unquestionably was a fine critic: his *W.B. Yeats* and *Varieties of Parable* prove that. Rodgers never seemed to have the inclination to write an extended critical piece and contented himself with reviews. I imagine that literary analysis would not, in any case, have been his *métier*. Rodgers wrote too little, MacNeice too much. But I prefer surplusage to its opposite both in prose and in poetry. Rodgers lacks a body of work to buttress his two volumes of poetry; MacNeice, with his wider range of interest and his journalistic flair, wrote more copiously (and facilely) and built his buttresses, even if some were on sand. I regret that Rodgers is now out of literary fashion. After all, Ireland is not so rich in poets as some people think. Rodgers does not deserve to be forgotten.

Louis MacNeice and Bertie Rodgers were migrants who arrived in Belfast once or twice a year, either singly or together, stayed for a few days, and then went off on their travels to England or Europe or beyond. Some of us always made a fuss of them as soon as they landed in Ireland, and the celebrations lasted until they left. The flat of the artists George and Mercy MacCann off Shaftesbury Square was one of their bases, its walls lined with pictures, some painted by George and Mercy themselves. There was also a Russian icon of which Mercy was very proud. The centre of the flat was a long refectory-like table in the dining room where their guests sat on chairs, stools or a bench and the bottles would move backwards and forwards and across like chessmen, as a stream of visitors arrived with bottles or were ordered to go out and fetch a bottle – or two if they felt like it – at the convenient off-licence in Botanic Avenue.

Belfast takes itself seriously, so seriously indeed that it has never paid much attention to its writers and artists. The numerous churches – and 'chapels', as the Catholic places of worship are called – may suggest that the inhabitants are religious-minded, and this I suppose is true, for both Catholics and Protestants take their faiths very seriously. But seriousness without tolerance in religious matters can prove dangerous to civilised living, and Belfast has never been otherwise than a dangerous and explosive city, a city from which writers and artists have fled, given the opportunity to do so.

The literary atmosphere appeared to be easier in Dublin, but this was largely illusory. A vicious censorship of books discouraged original creative work during the thirties and forties, and had to be vigorously fought by writers like Sean O'Faolain, Peadar O'Donnell, Frank O'Connor and others. We in the North had no literary censorship: still, the Dublin censors managed to catch Bell's *December Bride* in their capacious net: a decision which made Sam justly proud. He found himself in good company.

After the deaths of Yeats and Joyce, and with Bernard Shaw in old age and Sean O'Casey struggling with dramatic experiments and indefatigably continuing with his autobiography, the Irish contribution to world literature seemed to have reached exhaustion. Beckett, moving in a post-Joyce coterie in Paris, was still a minor figure; the most important writers left after the Second World War were O'Connor and O'Faolain in prose and

Austin Clarke and Patrick Kavanagh in poetry, all of them living, for the most part, in Dublin. The monthly publication of *The Bell* was their clarion call until it, too, exhausted its editors. With the Abbey under the tired direction of Lennox Robinson, the future of drama was bleak. Writers in the North, distanced politically and culturally from the South by the border, and isolated from England by the sea, felt denied, at least in part, their identity. It was impossible for us to fit into any English tradition even if we wanted to; so, though in permanent opposition to the fossilised Unionist government, a few flirted for a brief period with so-called regionalism, for which John Hewitt's persuasive voice was in search of recruits, until finally with the publication of *Lagan* and *Rann* each of us took his own way.

Sam Hanna Bell, as I have explained, joined the BBC; Michael McLaverty became headmaster of a Catholic school; Roy McFadden continued to practise law; Robert Greacen went to Dublin and then settled in London; John Hewitt left Belfast in anger against discrimination and took a job in Coventry; newcomers like Brian Friel, a teacher in Derry, Seamus Heaney, a teacher (under the aegis of McLaverty) in Belfast, Michael Longley, James Simmons, Derek Mahon and others appeared. Altogether something was stirring in the North, but exactly what would be the outcome of the sectarianism, the discrimination and the scab of unemployment that festered throughout the area we could only guess. Each writer I knew had his political stance: a Catholic was assumed to be a nationalist and a Protestant some kind of socialist or liberal. But few of us were actively engaged in political thinking, the exception being Denis Ireland, who for rejecting the political faith of his Protestant fathers had by now been rewarded with a seat in the Senate of the Republic. But Denis, unlike the rest of us, had a private income and could afford his independence. We admired him, of course, but also, I

102

think, we envied him. Andrew Boyd's political articles and pamphlets were more radical and down-to-earth, and therefore more to my own taste. He generously credited me with helping him to write his excellent Fabian pamphlet *The Two Irelands*. My only contribution to literary *engagement* in the North was an anonymous article in the *Times Literary Supplement*, which provoked a third leader in the *Belfast Telegraph*, much to my amusement, especially as the editor – my friend Jack Sayers – asked me who I thought the anonymous writer was. He never suspected me and of course I did not enlighten him. Bertie Rodgers had originally been invited to write the article but had passed it over to me. I cannot remember a word of what I wrote, but I do remember the secret pleasure I derived from writing this polemic. Strictly speaking, of course, I should have asked permission of the BBC to write this piece, but knowing my request might cause a fuss I chose not to do so.

I had a few friends inside Broadcasting House and many more outside. Inside we were a mixed lot, thrown together as if by chance, English, Scots and, of course Irish from both North and South. I never had much to do with the successive Controllers who arrived from London – aloof figures for the most part – who inhabited a huge office with a large table, a row of chairs for visitors, and a soft, leather sofa for their own comfort. A producer – even the Head of Programmes – was denied direct entry to this sanctum and instead had to approach it through the Controller's secretary's office where a chair was provided and admittance granted after a short waiting time. The only Controller I was on friendly terms with was Richard Marriott, who reigned in that office for only three years before his promotion to Director of Home Services in London. Richard was a tall, thin Englishman with dark, slightly unruly hair and a long inquisitive nose; he was shy, nervous, courteous, and extremely intelligent. One evening at about half past six, I met him on the stairs on his way out of the building. I think he had been only three weeks in Belfast and we began chatting in the hall. It suddenly occurred to me that the man was lonely and not looking forward to an empty evening in the Grand Central Hotel, where he was staying for the time being. He had scarcely yet ventured outside Belfast, except to take long walks to the surrounding hills. On an impulse I asked him whether he would like to take a drive to somewhere like Bangor. He accepted the offer so we turned towards the car park. It was the beginning of a friendship that lasted until his death. But the morning after this initial encounter, I was summoned to the office of the Head of Programmes.

'Was that the new Controller I saw in your car yesterday?' Harry McMullan began his inquisition.

'Yes, it was.'

'What was he doing in it?'

'We went for a drive.'

'How did this come about?'

I told him. He explained that this was a most irregular procedure. It was not to happen again. I accepted the reproof in silence and left the office. It happened that about a year later I received an invitation to be a member of an Irish delegation of writers and artists to the USSR, an invitation that required clearance. So I applied to Harry McMullan. As this was 1954 and the Cold War was still at its height I thought it doubtful that I should be permitted to join the delegation. Within a couple of days I was summoned to McMullan's office and told that I must reject the invitation, that the Controller had been consulted and could not possibly agree to my request. I refused to believe this and applied to Marriott himself, who consulted the appropriate London authority. A few days later McMullan again summoned me to his office and told me that he had persuaded the Controller to grant me leave of absence for the trip, adding that of course I would not be permitted to make any broadcasts in the USSR. As I had no intention of doing so I nodded my agreement to this restriction of my freedom.

Still, I had some colleagues whose company I enjoyed and who enjoyed my company. Sam Hanna Bell was the one I was closest to: he had even dedicated one of his novels to me (coupling my name with Jim Stewart's). I had introduced him to Mildred, the golden-haired schoolteacher who later became his wife. We had in common those holidays spent at Murlough Bay long before we had joined the BBC, and during my twenty-five years as a producer he and I often spent our lunchtimes together, buying second-hand books in Smithfield, borrowing books from the Linen Hall Library, or just wandering around the town gossiping. We shared an enthusiasm for Thomas Hardy, but perhaps taking our cue from MacNeice and Rodgers we usually avoided literary discussion; we were the two members of staff most interested in politics, both of us left-wingers.

Two allies – or so we considered them – were Edgar Boucher, who was in charge of music, and Moore Wasson, who was in charge of religious broadcasts. And during his short stay in Belfast John Gibson, a fervent young Scot, who produced drama, was added to our little group. Without these colleagues the BBC in Belfast would have been, at least for me, a dull place indeed. Some of the other members of staff, their eyes fixed on various promotional ladders, kept their mouths shut, firm believers in the value of discretion. I have sometimes wondered how much satisfaction their ambition brought. As for myself I was never denied promotion, simply because I never sought it. Richard Marriott once offered to find me a post in London, suggesting that the atmosphere there would be more liberal than

105

the parochialism of Belfast. He seemed disappointed and surprised when I decided not to accept his offer. In fact I never gave it serious thought, though I enjoyed London and had to go from time to time to attend meetings or to produce programmes. I knew what it had to offer – theatre, music, galleries, new friends – but somehow the baits did not appear to me enticing enough. Home was home. Belfast was Belfast. It was impossible for me to loosen the strings that bound me to the city. It was where I belonged and where I always would belong. And that is how it has been.

6

Conditions in the Six Counties were such that artists and writers had a habit of fleeing for their lives – and their art – to Dublin or to London.

St John Ervine was one who fled to London, and his career as a playwright, novelist, biographer and journalist brought him fame and fortune in his lifetime. A man of considerable talent, he somehow lost his way between Ireland and England – in contrast to his adored Bernard Shaw who found his way. My explanation for this is that Shaw held fast to an Irishness that Ervine as a young man adhered to proudly but lost in early middle age, with the consequence that his talent gradually withered.

His life was extraordinary. At the age of seventeen he arrived in London poor and friendless, a youngster from Ballymacarrett in Belfast, with hardly any education but with a driving ambition to succeed. He found a job in an insurance office, joined the Fabian Society, became acquainted with Shaw, had his first play, *Mixed Marriage*, accepted by the Abbey Theatre, and rose, like Shaw himself, by sheer ability.

I knew little of his life when I first met him, but when he learned that I too was brought up in Ballymacarrett, not far from his grandmother's shop on the Albertbridge Road, his memories of childhood poured out of him like a flood. He was then well over sixty, a carefully dressed, dignified man with a mop of abundant white wavy hair, and his face in repose had a stern expression; he reminded me of a Victorian patriarch. But when he took off his glasses after a bout of laughter – and he laughed readily and raucously – you would at once notice his squint. He was frail-looking, of medium height and handicapped by his artificial leg, which was the result of a wound sustained at the end of the First World War. He was blind in one eye and had only partial sight in the other, and he had a poor stomach. Yet whenever we spent a day together, at Honey Ditches, his home in south Devon, or in London or in Belfast, his good spirits were infectious. He loved an argument and was a formidable opponent. I once reminded him of the time he appeared on the BBC 'Brains Trust', when one of the speakers was C.E.M. Joad, the popular philosopher, who began displaying his knowledge of dramatic art by quoting from Aristotle's *Poetics*. Ervine suddenly interrupted Joad's discourse: 'Damn Aristotle! Damn Aristotle! What plays did he ever write?' Ervine had forgotten this incident, and commented, with a gale of laughter, 'Well, if I did say that, I only wanted to take the fella down a peg! He was very bumptious. Don't you think so?'

By this time I knew Ervine well enough to be blunt with him, and I reported that I had met a few people who thought him pretty bumptious too.

'Is that so?' he answered, a note of surprise in his voice. 'I wonder why is that? I can't understand why. You know, I'm a shy man ... very shy. Do I not appear to be so?'

'You certainly do not.'

'Well I am. I'm very nervous before an audience – whether in a hall or before a broadcast. But once I get started I suppose I'm all right ...'

He was an excellent lecturer and broadcaster, with a clear delivery, every word carefully enunciated. I think he modelled his speaking style on Shaw's, just as he modelled his prose on Shaw's. But neither in speech nor in writing did he measure up to his mentor. He was fully aware of course of the gap between Shaw's genius and his own talent, and immensely proud that 'G.B.S.' (as he always referred to him) had re-written the opening of *People of Our Class*. This comedy, despite Shaw's commendation of it as 'Chekhov in Devon', failed to find a producer and Ervine was bitterly disappointed. Still, he had his share of successes in the West End, and *Robert's Wife* was produced a couple of years later.

I admired him and liked him, but found it difficult to understand him and impossible to be sympathetic to many of his views. What I most admired in him was his courage: he said what he thought. He was not afraid of making enemies – and he made many – and he was even not afraid of making enemies of his friends, for he could be quick to take offence. Disputatious, unpredictable, cantankerous, and opinionated, Ervine sometimes seemed to invite abuse: he certainly gave it to others, including me. When I returned from the USSR and told him I was impressed by what I saw there his contempt was so scathing that he shouted, 'When on earth are you going to grow up! You're a bloody fool! You saw only what they wanted to show you! Are you a some kind of Bolshevik? Or worse, a fellow-traveller?' I pleaded guilty to sharing the opinions of Shaw and the Webbs, and guilty to believing that Marx and Engels and Lenin had made great contributions to world progress; I explained that I tried to keep an open mind as far as humanly possible, that I detested dogmatism and bigotry, that I did not allow the partiality of my political opinions to sway my judgements as a producer.

'You're a hopeless case,' he retorted. 'A hopeless case. I don't know what's going to become of you.'

I did not know myself what was going to become of me, and gave the matter hardly any thought. But whatever happened to me I knew I had no ambitions to follow in St John's footsteps. He was born plain John Ervine but adorned his name to the more decorative St John Ervine, probably because it sounded grander and because it was once a fashion in theatrical circles to drop common names and assume aristocratic ones. It is of course only a minor affectation, but it somehow jars.

St John greatly admired his adopted country and considered that England had given him his opportunities to become a writer. But if his admiration of England was just, his denigration of Ireland became an obsessional neurosis. He could see little good in his fellow countrymen and countrywomen and his spiteful attitude towards them is far from attractive. I think it stemmed from the rebellion in 1916, which he regarded as an act of treachery against a Britain engaged in a war for civilisation against barbarism. After a short but stormy interlude in 1915 as manager of the Abbey Theatre (which had given him his first chance as a playwright) he left Dublin in anger and in 1916 he joined the British Army, serving with the Royal Dublin Fusiliers in France until the leg wound that necessitated his artificial limb. He very seldom talked about his injury but I can recall one occasion on which he did. He was sitting at his desk in his sitting room at Honey Ditches and we were discussing Shaw, whose books were piled up on the desk for consultation.

'G.B.S. was uncommonly kind to me,' he said. 'He came to see me when I was convalescing in hospital after this happened to me.' He touched his leg gently. 'Yes, uncommonly kind.'

'Uncommonly is one of your favourite words,' I said.

'Is that so?' The memory of Shaw's kindness made his eyes flood with tears. 'I was, of course, full of self-pity, but G.B.S. soon cheered me up. He said to me, "When a tree is lopped it comes to no harm, does it? You've nothing to fear, St John. You'll be as right as rain." Then d'you know what he did? He took out his cheque book and gave me an open cheque. Wasn't that uncommonly kind?' He mimed Shaw's action, paused and continued: 'I burst into tears and took his hands in mine. I was very moved and he saw I was and he said, "What are you making a fuss about? I'll charge you my usual five per cent, you know!" Of course he didn't, but he had to have his little joke. Some fools say G.B.S. was mean and ungenerous. What nonsense! He was the most generous and kind man I ever met. Of course he attracted parasites ... many, many scroungers. You know, I hate and detest scroungers!'

Ervine himself was a kind and generous man, though his tongue could be vitriolic. When I told him of his reputation for prickliness he did not seem too upset at the charge.

'Well, if I give hard knocks I've had to take them too. I don't worry over such things. What's the harm in speaking out what's in your mind? I've called you more than once a bloody fool, haven't I?'

I admitted he had and that I did not in the least mind.

'You see, you don't mind. And you know why? You don't believe you are! Too high an opinion you have of yourself – if you ask me. Mebbe I'm just the same. I believe I am.'

It was knockabout good humour and Nora, his wife, would sit listening and smiling at her husband's performance, occasionally interrupting him when she thought he was being outrageous. 'Your tongue has got you into trouble more than once,

111

St John. And sometimes you regret what you've said. Isn't that true?'

'Never! Never! I can't remember ever regretting a word!' Then his loud laugh would follow.

I thought he should have regretted whole books he had written. His biography of Craigavon, the first premier of Northern Ireland, was in my view a disastrous book. He took about six years to write it and it attracted few readers; it was remaindered and deserved to be. I thought it one of the most ill-mannered and ill-considered books I had ever tried to read, and I failed to finish it. I was glad we never discussed it.

How the same person could choose to write biographies of Craigavon and of Shaw I find impossible to understand: Craigavon, a dull reactionary Ulsterman, and Bernard Shaw, whose literary achievement ranks him with the greatest Irishmen of all time. How anyone could come under the influence of Shaw and learn so little from him remains a mystery to me.

Indeed, Ervine himself remains something of an enigma. On one of his visits to Belfast he asked me to come with him to the Albertbridge Road. He wanted to see his grandmother's shop again and the streets where he had spent his childhood. He was unsure of the year and place of his birth, but his earliest memories were centred round this small hardware shop. On an earlier occasion – when I was staying at Honey Ditches – he confessed to me that both his parents had been deaf and dumb and that he retained no memories of either of them, though he possessed a small photograph of his mother. He opened a drawer of his desk and handed the photograph to me. It was of a young and beautiful woman. I handed it back to him and he said, 'All my memories are of my grandmother.'

Like Shaw, Ervine was an autodidact, but unlike Shaw, whose mother was a musician, Ervine had no cultural background at all; he was little more than an inquisitive schoolboy when he departed for London. And London made him – just as it made Shaw. Ervine's reputation declined towards the end of his life, and his once-fashionable plays became unfashionable. His book on Oscar Wilde was a destructive and mean-minded effort. Only his biography of Shaw won respect, written as it was from love of his subject.

When I last saw St John Ervine he was in his mid-eighties and living in a private nursing home in Hampshire. In old age he had retained his looks, his halo-like white hair and his erect posture; we chatted for about an hour in the dining room over cups of tea and biscuits. He was in good spirits and often burst into laughter at my remarks. But towards the end of our meeting he suddenly asked, 'Where did you say you came from?'

'From Belfast.'

That news seemed to give him pleasure and he said, 'You know, I was born there.'

'Yes, St John, I know you were.'

'I love Donaghadee. That's the place I would like to be.'

'You've always loved Donaghadee.'

'How did you know that?'

'You told me often enough.'

'Did I?'

I chattered on for a while about Donaghadee but he only smiled, and asked me no further questions. I thought it was time for me to go, as I did not wish to exhaust him. I rose and told him that I was returning to London. We shook hands and I knew I would never see him again.

'You live in London?' he asked me.

'No. In Belfast.'

He was silent and let my hand fall. 'In Belfast?'

I nodded. He looked at me as if puzzled.

113

'Don't you know who I am?' I asked.

He shook his head.

The matron thanked me for coming to see him and said that he had few visitors. Then she told me that he was very quiet and read a little every day.

'Yes,' I said. 'He's been a great reader all his life.'

About a year afterwards he died, but where he is cremated or buried I have never bothered to find out. Somehow it did not seem to matter. I assumed it was somewhere in England. He ought to have been buried in Donaghadee in his beloved County Down.

The plays of St John Ervine, George Shiels and Joseph Tomelty made up the staple diet of the Ulster Group Theatre, which was a kind of annexe of the Ulster Hall where, from long before I was born, all the great political rallies took place. Winston Churchill had once taken the platform there, and after his oration had to flee from angry Ulster Protestants who, if they had caught hold of him, would have made him the sorry man. Or so I was told. But what Churchill said to annoy his audience I never learned. My Granda Leeman's comment when I asked for the reason for the near-riot was terse. 'Ach, that oul' turncoat of an Englishman is no better nor a Home Ruler!'

I was a regular patron of the Group but not always an enthusiastic one. Too many kitchen comedies were produced on that cramped little stage to suit my taste. I was hungry for Ibsen and Shaw and Chekhov, three dramatists the Group audiences for the most part looked on with suspicion. I, of course, looked on the audiences with equal suspicion as being philistines who attended the theatre only for laughs.

Two of my uncles, Willie and Tommy, both of them patrons of the Group and both fervent socialists, agreed with me that kitchen comedies could become tiresome and that the working class should have the opportunity of seeing more of the 'heavy stuff', preferably with a 'message' to lead the workers in the direction of socialism. Shaw was their favourite dramatist, and if they had lived to experience the plays of Brecht he too would have been their man, especially with a play like *The Mother*.

As the Group was about a hundred yards from the BBC, Sam Bell and I used to call at the box office for chats with Joe Tomelty, who was then in the prime of his career, before his almost fatal car accident in England prevented him from realising all his potentialities as actor, playwright and novelist. Joe possessed the knack of writing light comedies that won the approval of the Group audiences, but more than once, as an actor, he found it necessary to discipline his audience by ordering them to stop chattering and give more of their attention to the play. Like my two uncles, Joe took the theatre to be more than a noisy place of entertainment. He aspired to write serious drama – *All Souls' Night* is proof of that – but his gift for farce and comedy sidetracked his serious aspirations; *All Souls' Night* stands out clearly from his dozen or more other plays as his most ambitious achievement.

The Group produced a remarkable crop of actors, including R. H. MacCandless, J. G. Devlin, Harold Goldblatt, Stephen Boyd, Elizabeth Begley, Margaret D'Arcy and many others, but no outstanding directors or designers. And certainly no outstanding dramatists. Ervine and Shiels were too well established in their careers for the Group to claim them, and Tomelty's career was cut short by his accident. The Group collapsed after a three-year row concerning a play by a new playwright, Sam Thompson, a painter from the Belfast shipyards, who had the audacity to write about the bigotry and sectarianism he had first-hand experience of in his workplace.

Thompson's play *Over the Bridge* split the board of directors of the Group, was finally produced in early 1960 at the Empire Theatre, and turned out to be a huge success: the liberals won a victory which is still remembered by those of us who care for the survival of serious theatre in Northern Ireland. Still, the Group despite its ignominious end and its limitations and drawbacks – no subsidies, a hall not built as a theatre and the dressing rooms primitive – was a gallant venture while it lasted. And at least it brought Sam Thompson to the fore, even if it had to commit hari-kiri as a consequence.

I always associated Thompson with Sam Hanna Bell who, as an established writer and radio producer, gave Thompson much encouragement and practical help. Their rendezvous was the Elbow Room and from their wild, woolly and at times incoher-ent discussions there some ideas usually survived: a pub is a better place for the germination of imaginative ideas than any BBC office. I can remember spending only one long drinking session with Sam Thompson, which was to discuss an idea he had for a short story. For some reason he suggested that we meet in a pub behind the Ormeau Baths. It was empty in the early afternoon and remained empty while Thompson talked about his story and finally plucked up courage to read it in a low voice, glancing up now and again to see the effect it was having on me. I did not give my decision on it until I had had a chance to read it myself; a couple of days later we met in my office and I told him that I could not accept his story in its present form, that he would have to rewrite it. He was crestfallen and for a long time afterwards avoided me, numbering me among his enemies. Whether if he had persisted he would have become a short-story writer I do not know; certainly his first effort was poor, but then nearly all first efforts in this subtle art are failures. I thought afterwards that the failure was just as much mine as his. Writers are vulnerable creatures even at the best of times when they appear to have confidence in themselves and have already done good work; a beginner like Sam Thompson, with all the diffidence of someone with the minimum of education, should have been treated by me with more patience and understanding. As a result of my failure, he and I never became close friends, which I regret. But if I never won his friendship I think he realised later that I was far from being his enemy: and he had at least one in the BBC whom he would have gladly lynched.

Sam Thompson never made much money by his writing. He died young at thirty-nine, the same age as did Dylan Thomas. And he died conscious that his literary career had really only begun with his two plays *Over the Bridge* and *The Evangelist*. Both have technical defects, but both have a vitality, a forcefulness, a sense of conviction that make them superior to better crafted efforts by experienced playwrights. Tyrone Guthrie once said to me, 'We should cherish Sam Thompson.' And Guthrie himself did precisely that.

I believe that Sam Thompson would have become a considerable playwright if he had been given enough time to study his art, and if the theatre in Belfast had not been so frightened to present the reality of local industrial conditions and relationships. Sam knew at first hand what he was writing about, and middle-class theatregoers did not want to know. Thousands of workers did, and they packed the Empire week after week, in a kind of theatrical explosion comparable, I think, to what happened in the Abbey with the early plays of O'Casey. O'Casey spent an apprenticeship learning his craft before *The Shadow of a Gunman*, *Juno and the Paycock* and *The Plough and the Stars* were ready for the Dublin audiences. These extraordinary plays aroused controversy of course, especially *The Plough and the Stars*, but the Abbey, headed by Yeats and Lady Gregory, won their fight and the Irish theatre recognised a new dramatic genius. Though Belfast had no Yeats or Lady Gregory, Sam Thompson certainly had his supporters and *Over the Bridge* has survived the fainthearts. I imagine it will survive as long as sectarianism divides the people of the North of Ireland, and longer.

The most authoritative theatrical figure in the North lived across the political border in the South: Tyrone Guthrie's home was Annaghmakerrig, near Newbliss in County Monaghan. Guthrie, an internationally famous director, was better known in England and in America than in Ireland, North or South. He was a big man both physically and – I once thought – intellectually. Standing nearly six and a half feet tall, with a chiselled face whose dominant feature was his large beaklike nose, Guthrie towered over whatever company he was in. At his side someone as short as I seemed to belong to a different species, and walking together was something of an ordeal for me, unused as I was to trotting as a form of exercise.

The theatre was his life, and from his undergraduate days at Oxford to his sudden death at his desk at home at Annaghmakerrig it obsessed him.

But though he believed passionately in the importance of drama and devoted himself to directing plays in various parts of the world, to planning new theatres, to writing plays and writing about plays, Guthrie was not satisfied with the life of make-believe, with the dramatic experience in its many forms. He was acutely concerned with social problems but not as a sociologist or as a politician, simply as a human being and a Christian who wished to help better the lives of the people in his neighbourhood. To this end he started up a jam factory in a disused railway station, employing local unemployed workers and selling the jam himself in New York or Belfast or wherever he happened to be directing plays. It was good jam and he was

118

proud of it, singing its virtues to his friends and persuading them to buy it. When I once asked him to broadcast a talk on drama he replied, 'No, dear boy, not again. Can't you think up something else for a change?'

'What's on your own mind, Tony?'

'Jam, jam, jam! Let me broadcast about the making of jam.'

'But you can't advertise your own jam factory, that's forbidden, as you well know.'

'I don't intend to advertise, dear boy, merely to eulogise.'

He wrote his radio talk; it was accepted by the World Service, and if it was not an advertisement for Newbliss jam I do not know what it was. I do know it was a superb talk delivered with all his brio.

I believe he saw himself as the Chekhov of County Monaghan: just as Chekhov was a doctor as well as a writer so Guthrie felt himself to be more than a man of the theatre. He loved his home at Annaghmakerrig, with its gardens, its woods and the beautiful lake a mile long which as a young man he had swum from end to end. He enjoyed having guests to stay and they came from many countries. I well remember the first time I arrived there and stood looking at the lake, the woods and the house itself (which was really a large farmhouse, with no architectural pretensions).

'Chekhov!' I exclaimed. *'The Seagull.'*

'I'm glad you didn't say Turgenev,' he replied.

He and his wife Judith (they could have been brother and sister, they resembled each other so much) were perfect hosts. When he invited me to stay for a long weekend he thought it advisable to give a warning. 'Nothing to do, dear boy. *At all.* No entertainments *at all.* No wireless, no newspapers. Plenty of books. Good walking. You mightn't see much of Judith or m'self – except possibly at meals.' Annaghmakerrig was indeed restful;

idyllic. I do not even recall reading a book there, though three or four carefully chosen books were always placed on a chair near my bed; the room was simplicity itself. The meals, too, were simple, the only luxury a bottle of wine. In the evenings we would have an after-dinner chat and then it was early to bed.

One evening he suggested I should read aloud a documentary programme I had compiled and brought with me to complete. It was a pedestrian affair and sounded exactly that. He suggested that I might like to listen to something he had written. He read beautifully as always, making me all too conscious of the stiltedness of my own delivery. His script was on a biblical theme, but what it was I cannot recall; I was sitting in an armchair in front of a great log fire, exhausted with the nervous effort of my own reading and wondering how inept and amateurish it must have sounded compared with the professionalism of his own reading. Made drowsy by the heat of the fire, the after-effects of a good meal and the roll of the biblical rhythms, I found it hard to keep my eyes open and was nearly asleep when he finished.

'Beautiful,' I said, knowing that some response was called for; I had nothing more to offer other than the repetition of the word. Judith came to my rescue and made a few technical comments, which he accepted with his elongated 'Yass ... Yaas ... Yaas.'

Guthrie called his autobiography *A Man of the Theatre*, and though I have read it I have never been tempted to re-read it, which is the only test I have of whether I am really interested in a book; I found his autobiography surprisingly dull. Dull, because Guthrie never gives himself away: he records and observes, like a stage director casting and interpreting a play; he himself is not on the stage but somewhere in the semi-darkness of the auditorium, deeply involved with the drama but not with the drama of self. I suspect that Guthrie, despite his talent, his culture and his zest for life, failed to create something of permanent worth. He would liked to have written a great play. His verbose *Top of the Ladder* was his attempt and it is a failure; indeed, it is an embarrassing failure.

I saw *Top of the Ladder* in the middle of its short run at the St James's theatre in London in 1951. Guthrie directed and John Mills played the protagonist Bertie, a middle-aged prosperous businessman. The performances have faded from my memory but the play itself was diffuse and over-ambitious, a pretentious effort. When I read Guthrie's programme note I thought his approach to his play disastrously ill-conceived. He wrote: 'The play is much concerned with symbols: key, box, ladder, window, railway, river, garden, and so on. All are intended to convey a shadow-meaning larger but vaguer than their literal meaning.' He then invoked 'humbly and reverentially' three particular shadows – James Frazer, James Joyce, Sigmund Freud. Predictably a mishmash.

Guthrie once confessed to me that he was no judge of a good play, a remark I took as modesty but later decided was true. We seldom discussed drama but I remember challenging his estimate of James Bridie, whom he judged to be a greater dramatist than Bernard Shaw. I considered this nonsense and reproached him for it; he brushed my objections aside with an abrupt 'Well, I may be wrong.' I may have been foolish in rushing to the defence of Shaw (who needs no defending, by me or anybody else) for the occasion was an article contributed to the *Listener* on the death of Bridie, an occasion when exaggeration is excusable, especially from a generous-minded friend.

I have hardly mentioned Judith, a tall and often smiling figure who kept her place discreetly behind her famous husband; when I visited their home alone my attention was mostly directed towards her husband, but when Elizabeth, my wife, was with me the balance was preserved. Once I asked Judith if she would be willing to broadcast a book review and she agreed provided her talk could be recorded. So I went to Annaghmakerrig with a portable tape-recording machine and after a couple of false starts – and the necessary drink to fortify confidence – the review was successfully taped. It was an ordeal, Judith frankly confessed, and she sighed her relief when it was over. We were alone in the library (for Tony had gone to London) and I was surprised that she had been so nervous during the recording. I realised then that she had been playing a role to which she was unaccustomed, and that without her husband she felt insecure and vulnerable. Nearly always he was by her side to give her moral support, and with him present – or even near at hand – all would be well. A further complication had been that the novel I had sent her was one that she felt unfitted to review. It was Benedict Kiely's *At Night All Cats are Grey*. As I myself had not read it before sending it off to her I had to ask her about it.

'Wasn't it good?'

'Oh yes, excellent. But it was very sexy, very sexy indeed.'

I had made a careless mistake and had chosen the wrong reviewer. Despite my mistake Judith had managed to write a sympathetic review of Kiely's novel, but nevertheless she found the experience an unhappy one and had no wish to repeat it, unless of course I was able to find the right book for her. I never did.

Guthrie was recognised as one of the outstanding broadcasters of his time and it was one of my greatest pleasures to produce him. In fact he required no production at all: his script had only to be timed. He was equally good in an unscripted discussion. For years I naïvely assumed that Guthrie's artistry as a speaker came naturally, without much self-rehearsal, but I discovered that my assumption was wrong. His artistry was the result of experience, of training his voice by singing methods and by practice and hard work. He was an exponent of radio as a medium – particularly radio drama where he was a pioneer with plays like *Squirrel's Cage* – but he also convinced himself that 'canned' programmes in film and radio form would oust stage plays, and that theatregoing would become, like polo, a pleasure attainable only by the rich. He was partly right, of course: the theatre has survived, though as a minority art, and television is now the dominant medium. He would, I think, have been as successful in his directing of television as he was in radio and on stage. But he was too old and too tired to make a new start. Towards the end of his life he was conscious that he had passed his peak in the theatre and that younger men had overtaken him and usurped his position. However, as a performer on television he was superb and I was lucky enough to be his producer in a notable straight-to-camera programme recorded by Radio Telefís Éireann in Dublin at the beginning of the Troubles.

On one occasion we met in the early evening an hour before we were due in the Belfast studios to make a recording of his favourite poetry and prose. This personal anthology was expected to embrace a wide selection of work but for some reason Guthrie had been mulish with me when we had talked over the brief in Annaghmakerrig a few weeks before.

'Tell me exactly what you wish me to do,' he had asked.

'I'd like you to select three or four passages of memorable prose and perhaps four or five lyrics, and link them together with a commentary. That's all.'

'Well, that's quite simple,' he had replied. 'I'll chose all my favourite passages from the Bible.'

'That's too simple – and too easy,' I retorted. 'This isn't intended to be a religious programme.'

'But that's what I'd like to do. I'm extremely fond of reading the Bible.'

'I know you are. But you've read some other books, haven't you?' I said dryly.

'You tell me what they are then.'

I rolled out the names of writers he must have read or mentioned to me. Swift? Dickens? Wordsworth? Yeats? Forster? Forrest Reid?

'Yaas ... Yass ... Yass.'

'It's not my anthology, Tony, it's yours, remember.'

'Yass ... Yass ... I understand.'

So, obedient as ever to his producer, he had prepared his script, and it corresponded to the brief of the programme. Our rehearsal for the recording was brief, even briefer than usual, for I knew he liked to give a fresh and spontaneous performance. All went well, as always with him, and we crossed the road to the Elbow Room for a drink. I thought he looked tired.

'How did you spend the day, Tony?'

'I went up to the hills,' he said, a biblical cadence in his voice.

'And is that where you've been until we met for our meal?'

'Yes, I like to spend a long time in the country, alone.'

'So you'd no lunch?'

'No.' He explained that he had taken the car up into the Holywood Hills and spent the morning and afternoon rehearsing himself.

A short time after this programme I learned that Guthrie was a patient in the Royal Victoria Hospital with cardiac trouble; I was told that he did not wish to receive visitors. It so happened that Diana Hyde, a colleague of mine and a friend of Guthrie's, was also a patient in the Royal at the same time. So I went to visit her and she told me she had already seen Guthrie and had brought him some fruit. So I entered his private ward. The door was wide open; he lay in his pyjamas on top of the bed, his thin, storklike legs stretching far beyond the end of the bed. He was reading and did not hear me enter, so I stood for a moment or two half wishing that I had not come and feeling that my instinct to intrude on him was mistaken. He looked up from his book, and stared at me with his mouth open. Then he drew up his legs and greeted me with a welcoming smile. 'Ah, dear boy, how good to see you! How did you know I was here?'

'I heard a rumour, Tony. Belfast, you know, is really a village. Rumours fly round all the time.' I remember Guthrie was reading one of Jane Austen's novels with great pleasure and I wondered why he had not included her in the personal anthology he had recently recorded. But I did not raise that subject and it occurred to me that he was probably feeling unwell on that occasion. We chatted for a short while and he made me promise to come and see him at Annaghmakerrig.

This encounter brought home to me for the first time that Guthrie, who always looked so tall, his back straight, his head tilted high, his aquiline nose sniffing the air like some animal's, was not the earthly god he appeared to be but a mere mortal and heir to the body's ailments. When he recovered he made a six weeks' or so recuperative sea voyage to Australia, during which he enjoyed the new experience of teaching English to Italian immigrants and read a book on early Irish art which I had given him. He loved the vitality of Australians and directed *Oedipus* in Sydney; he wrote telling me that he had met Patrick White and recommended me to read his novels. When Guthrie returned home he seemed a rejuvenated man.

7

The three weeks I spent in the USSR in January 1956 were the most exhilarating weeks of my life. The visit was a cloak-and-dagger affair from the start, and it began one evening in the Elbow Room when my friend Stephen Wynburne introduced me to a quiet, stocky man whose name I have forgotten. Over drinks Stephen suddenly said to me in his precise voice, 'If you'd like a free trip to the USSR it can be arranged.' He smiled and indicated the quiet stocky man sitting opposite us, who gave a slight smile and said, 'Yes, it can be arranged.'

'Who can arrange it?' I asked.

'I can,' he answered. 'Without any difficulty.'

'There you are,' said Stephen. 'It's a good offer, isn't it?'

I am much too cautious and sceptical by nature to accept 'good offers' at their face value, whether in a shop window during a sale or propaganda by a political party. I did not relish being taken for a ride and made to feel foolish afterwards. So I had questions to ask and answers to weigh before I could come to a decision to accept or reject this tempting offer.

I had the greatest respect for Wynburne, who was an ex-colleague of mine at the Royal Academy, where he had taught

French and English. Later he became a lecturer at Stranmillis teacher training college. Stephen was a tall, pale, slightly stooped, scholarly man who dressed conventionally, was abstemious, loved sports – particularly rugby football – and was a conscientious teacher and a reliable friend. Outwardly the most conventional of men, inwardly he was most unconventional. He was a communist by conviction, though not a member of the Communist Party; he had been to the USSR and seen much to admire there, but he was far from being an uncritical admirer of any country, creed or political organisation. He had graduated from Trinity College Dublin at the same time as Samuel Beckett, and had come second to him in his finals. He remembered Beckett well. So when Stephen recommended a course of action to me I was inclined to follow his advice. The snag was whether I was in a position to do so. But as I have already explained, Richard Marriott had confidence in my professional integrity and cleared the way for my visit.

It began badly. Our group of seven – three from the North, four from the South – met in a London pub to begin our journey across the so-called Iron Curtain. Immediately I entered the pub and was introduced to my fellow travellers from Dublin and Belfast I learned that the trip was off. The explanations I was given were so muddled and the mood of the little group was so morose – some had already taken to drink in despair – that my first reaction was one of anger.

'How did this happen?' I asked.

'Ach, them eejits in Dublin don't know what they're at!'

'Who are *they*?'

'I can't tell you because I don't know. Peadar O'Donnell is mixed up in it.'

'No, he's not! It's some other fella!'

'Who's the other fella?'

'I don't know. I never met him.'

'How do you know the trip's off?' I asked.

'We've been in touch with the Russian Embassy. They told us.'

'What did they tell you?'

'Somebody there answered the telephone and told us we'd to make our way to Prague.'

'To *Prague*?'

'Where the hell is Prague? What country?'

'I dunno.'

'How could we get there anyway?'

'This is a balls-up.'

'How can we get home?'

'On the boat we came on.'

'I couldn't show m' face in Dublin after this, could you?'

'Jasus no, how could I?'

'We'll all be a laughin' stock.'

I had a whiskey and felt that I too was in this imbroglio and that I must try to get out of it. I had been granted my summer holiday for four weeks in January and here I was in a London pub with six other Irishmen – two writers, a sculptor, an architect and two journalists – marooned and miserable and beginning to spend the little money we had on drink. Through the babble of voices I learned that the others, like myself, had been told not to bring more than £10 in our pockets, that we would need no more. I knew I could get a bed for the night at 64 St George's Square, the ground-floor two-room flat where the writer Bill Naughton lived, for Bill could be relied on to give me all he had – accommodation, food, a few quid, and above all a laugh and a welcome – and so I had nothing to worry about for the immediate future. Bill himself might be broke but that would not matter – he would find a friend who was not and all would be well. I had another drink, then decided to drink no more but to use the telephone.

Someone mentioned that Pat Sloan, a well-known writer on Soviet affairs, might be able to give us some advice. I rang him and he advised us to try the Soviet Embassy again, and not to give up. He also told us that he knew of a Soviet ship that was due to leave the London docks that evening. We should try to get on board: the Russians would take care of us. Had we any money for a single voyage to the USSR border? If we did not, he would accept a cheque from me provided I had enough money lodged in my bank to cover the single fares of the group of seven. I explained to Sloan that I had no chequebook with me. What was the name of my bank, he wanted to know. I told him the Northern Bank. He had never heard of it. Well, he would accept an IOU from me written on any old scrap of paper. Had I any paper, he enquired. Yes, an old envelope. That would do, he assured me. He would meet us at the dockside, but in the meantime, go to the Soviet Embassy at once before it closed for the day. At once. He himself would speak to the Ambassador. Everything would be arranged.

And miraculously it was. We went to the embassy, saw a first secretary, explained our predicament, and told him that the reputation of the Soviet Union in Ireland was at stake. He nodded, and the Ambassador himself appeared briefly, shook hands with us and disappeared with a wide smile. It was five o'clock. The Soviet ship was to sail with the tide at six o'clock. It seemed too late to catch it, and anyway we had no visas to enter the USSR nor had we tickets to get on board the ship. Our group became dispirited and one or two wanted to return to the pub. I argued that that would be a mistake and was at once elected chairman of the delegation. I suggested we take a couple of taxis to the docks. It seemed a silly suggestion but at least it was better than going back to our pub and getting drunk. Maybe Pat Sloan would turn up.

He did not. We stood on the dockside, a disconsolate, huddled little group apparently bereft of friends and helpers, betrayed by somebody or other in Dublin, somebody indifferent to what our fates might be. Our only consolation was that the time was well after six and the Soviet ship still stood tantalising us at the dock, ready to depart at any moment. And we stood, without visas or embarkation tickets, looking at her longingly, like children gazing at some expensive toy in a shop window just outside their reach.

Suddenly two taxis appeared. Four men rushed out and joined us. My IOU for £120 was handed over, embarkation tickets were distributed, then visas, we found ourselves on board the Baltic State Steamship Line vessel *Estonia*, which we were told had been held up for us, and we were on our way down the Thames to the Soviet Union. We asked what port the ship was destined for but nobody seemed to know: the only answer was a shrug and a gesture. One seaman suggested Leningrad but he was uncertain, and a woman crew member with bleached hair said, 'Closed: ice,' smiled and hurried away, too busy to deal with our anxieties.

'We're here because we're here,' one of our group said grimly.

We stood on deck for a while, until somebody discovered a small bar and called out the good news.

Leningrad was indeed icebound and we disembarked at Riga, where a small group of children were waiting on the quayside, each carrying a bouquet of flowers. Much to our surprise the flowers were presented to us. It was a good beginning but we all felt embarrassed: it was curious to be treated like royalty in such circumstances. Then followed a meal in a banqueting hall, speeches, and glimpses of Riga in the wintry darkness on our way to the railway station and the train for Moscow. We had been allocated first-class compartments with bunks; there was a samovar at one end of the corridor and a Russian guide to look after us. He told me that he had arrived in Riga from Moscow only that morning, and had never visited the city before. He was shortish, plump, cheerful, with a large scar on the lower part of his face which he later explained was the result of a war wound; his jaw had been broken and it took so many months to heal that he began to study English, even though he had no knowledge of any foreign language when he began. When war was over he had become a guide. No, he had never been abroad, he told us, but had learned from records; he hoped some day to visit England. Ireland, too, we suggested. Yes, of course Ireland too. Why not? This phrase 'Why not?' recurred often during the next three weeks when one of us suggested going to a theatre, or a gallery, or a collective farm, or even the republic of Georgia. Our guide was not a handsome man but he was hardworking, with pleasant, open manners, though he was unable to smile because of his old wound.

The train to Moscow was slow and there were many stopping places in the middle of nowhere. A couple of times we got off to stretch our legs. Once, for an hour or so, I left our part of the train and travelled 'hard' where the seats were wooden and the heat and the stench were so overpowering that I thought I would faint. We were travelling 'privileged class' and in comfort, but there was no dining car. Our guide produced chunks of black bread and cheese and butter and we had a kind of picnic, washed down by large cups of tea with lemon.

Travelling into the heart of the USSR in midwinter by a nontourist route delighted me; it was as if the great nineteenth-century Russian novelists, Tolstoy and Gogol and Turgenev and the rest, had been resurrected as the vast bleak plains covered with falling snow unrolled endlessly before us, hour after hour. I had become friendly with Jim Plunkett, the only novelist in our party, and we both felt that just to experience the background against which these classical tales had been set more than compensated us for all the bother and fuss we had endured in London. Jim, a trade-union secretary as well as a writer, had already incurred criticism for having accepted the invitation to join the delegation to the USSR and he was worried that he might lose his job. I told him that I had no worries on that score, though my own joining of the delegation had caused some lifting of eyebrows in Belfast.

'Ach, Dublin's worse,' Jim contended. 'It's the Church, of course ... atheism an' all that. As soon as we get to Moscow, I'm goin' to find a Catholic Church or the nearest thing to it. And if we can only get a photograph of the lot of us at prayer all will be well.'

'But I'm not a Catholic, Jim.'

'What's it matter? You'll go too, won't you?'

'You want to get me, too, into trouble? Is that your plan?'

As soon as we reached Moscow, Jim asked to attend a Catholic service and on a Sunday we all trooped along accompanied by a Moscow photographer, surly, shabby and silent, who reminded me of a Belfast press photographer I knew who passed most of his waking hours in a pub off Royal Avenue. The church was packed, mostly with old, tired-looking women, but with a few men, including a Red Army soldier and a sprinkling of children, who were better dressed than the adults. The bored photographer took photographs, including one of me kneeling at prayer, a pietistic look on my face, which appeared in a Dublin newspaper much to the amusement of Jim Plunkett, who may well have been responsible for having me selected for special attention. I think the church was Polish, but whatever it was it satisfied the Dubliners and I found the service very moving, despite my unbelief. Our guide had brought along a young woman from VOKS, the organisation responsible for cultural contacts with foreigners, who looked on cheerfully and told me that she had never before attended a religious service. She commented, with a shrug, 'Backward people.' When I explained that most people in Ireland attended places of worship she gave a wry smile and enquired what my own religious belief was.

'None,' I replied.

'Good. Like myself. You belong to the Party?'

'No.'

'Intelligentsia?'

'Yes, I suppose so.' If I had to be labelled I could hardly take exception to the term 'intellectual', even though I was not sure I deserved it; but when she learned that I was a university graduate and had been a teacher she insisted I should classify myself as a member of the intelligensia. I had always thought of myself as more of a learner – and sometimes not too bright a one – but the young Russian was adamant about my classification.

It proved impossible in Moscow to assimilate more than a fraction of all that we saw and were told. Staying at the old-fashioned National Hotel facing the Kremlin we could have been visitors at the time of Tolstoy, but riding on the splendid Metro we were like ordinary Soviet citizens going about their daily business. One thing we all agreed on: our hosts had set out to please us and were succeeding.

Moscow, Sukhumi on the Black Sea, Tbilisi in Georgia, Leningrad: we travelled by rail, by air, by boat, by taxi. It was the most luxurious holiday I ever spent, and the longer I stayed in the USSR the more impressed I was by the country and its people. I did not arrive starry-eyed, and I did not leave starry-eyed: but I did leave deeply impressed and eager to learn more about 'the great experiment' – I think the phrase belongs to H.G Wells. I had read a good deal of the literature *pro* and *contra* the USSR and had sometimes been irritated and discomfited by what I read, but I was convinced beyond doubt that millions of people were undergoing a profound change in social organisation, that they had made tragic mistakes but had also made almost super-human achievements. That is neither an illuminating nor an original judgement, but no matter. The truth is that very few people have been able to study the USSR and it is disgraceful that a great work of scholarship like E.H. Carr's *History of Soviet Russia* is not more widely known. Most of the British and Irish 'intelligensia' have never heard of it. The Webbs may have had better luck with their *Soviet Communism* but their study, unlike Carr's, was not the result of a lifetime's study.

One cannot get to know any country from a short stay, especially not a vast continent like the USSR. It is surely possible to get the wrong impression of a place, even from sitting in a restaurant or on a bench in a park. Once I took a rest on a park bench in the midst of a crowd of about three hundred Russians, hoping to observe them at close quarters. My first, momentary, impression was that this crowd was more gesticulatory and altogether much more volatile than an ordinary Russian crowd. My puzzlement was shortlived. I had sat down in the midst of a gathering place for deaf mutes, all of them excited at seeing one another and eagerly communicating in their sign language. I felt as if I were abnormal, endowed as I was with the faculties of voice and hearing, both superfluous among these people, who seemed so vivacious without either faculty.

I spent a few hours wandering about on my own just as I liked to do in Dublin, London or Paris. I knew the Cyrillic alphabet, half a dozen phrases and a string of useful nouns. It was enough, if not to make me feel at home, at least to bring me into some kind of relationship with Russians. In their eyes I was at least a trier. Yet I made a poor tourist, for the sights often bored me. The Kremlin and the Hermitage are wonderful but my feet were sore. For me, the pleasure of looking at precious ornaments palls very quickly. I like to concentrate on two or three pictures at most: two or three thousand give me little pleasure. Excess bores. One of the best hours I spent in Moscow was in a second-hand bookstall somewhere in Arbat Street where I picked up a copy of Tolstoy's *Resurrection* in Russian and *The Financier* by Theodore Dreiser in English. I then took a crowded bus back to the National, standing for a moment, before a boy of about ten vacated his seat and indicated that I should take it. I thanked him saying '*Spasiba*', the word I probably used most during my stay.

What impressed me most I find hard to say, certainly not the discussion we had with Russian writers in the Writers' Union. This was a rambling discussion which ran aimlessly on parallel lines about different forms of censorship. The evening I most enjoyed was spent watching Mussorgsky's *Khovanshchina* at the Bolshoi: an unforgettable experience which I re-create from records. And there was the Kirov Ballet in Leningrad, the beauty of Georgian women and girls in Tbilisi, the sight of the Caucasus Mountains from the air in the morning light, the friendliness of farmers in Sukhumi, a walk along the Nevsky Prospeck in Leningrad. And there was the forgiveness of a sturdy middle-aged woman at a banquet in Moscow when one of our delegation, aiming the contents of a glass of wine across the table at a fellow Dubliner, missed his target and spoiled our hostess's beautiful blue dress. I apologised to her on behalf of our delegation; she made light of the incident, calling it a mistake and of no importance. It was, to us. We were ashamed.

We saw nothing of the dark side of the Soviet Union.

This visit to the USSR coloured the rest of my life to a shade of red, sometimes pale, sometimes bright. It also cemented my friendship with Stephen Wynburne, who was a quiet rebel like myself. Stephen's nonconformity exercised itself in the lecture rooms of Stranmillis College, where he was an isolated figure propagating the necessity for a revolution in the teaching of English. Basic English, the simplified form of English developed by C.K. Ogden, was his panacea for what he called 'diseased' languages, and day after day as we walked up and down the Ormeau Road or along the Lagan embankment or into the leafy quiet of Belvoir Park he would repeat into my half-reluctant ears the messianic message of Ogden and I.A. Richards. He walked smartly like the old soldier he was, and I sometimes wondered why he had never become an officer. He possessed all the attributes: the right accent, the superior education, the social manners, the interest in sport; but promotion was denied him, probably because of his political views. Whatever the reason, he never seemed to mind and never mentioned the subject to me. Language and its difficulties, rather than politics and its divisions, obsessed his acute intellect. As we walked along trying to tease out linguistic puzzles, I noticed that he was never at ease unless we walked in step, and if we did not he would give a little hop until we were in step again. Only then could his argument be continued.

'I cannot say, "The cat is on the mat",' he would repeat.
'Why not? You've just said it, haven't you?'
'I have. But it has no meaning. It is nonsense. Non-sense.'
'Why?'
'Because it has no context.'
'But if we give it a context –'
'Ah, then …'
With the years Stephen's advocacy of Basic English became so

repetitive that he began to bore his friends. His book *Vertical Translation*, which he published at his own expense, failed to bring about the revolution in teaching English that he enthusiastically championed. It is a valuable book, though it may be a long time before its value is recognised. But Stephen, like Samuel Beckett, faced apparent failure with equanimity, and though a rationalist – he called himself a scientific humanist – he was also a man of faith, and until his dying day in 1980 he proclaimed his faith in Basic English. He inscribed his book to me as one 'who knows as I do the truth of Proverbs 13:15. "Good understanding giveth favour: but the way of transgressors is hard."' Wynburne's life may be seen as a failure: he died an obscure academic in an uncongenial teaching establishment where his ideas for teaching English were not even considered of sufficient importance to be frowned upon; they were simply ignored by his fellow academics. So his only outlets were to write the occasional article (usually rejected) for a newspaper, give a lecture to a local society, or bore his few friends with his linguistic ideas. He seldom bored me, however, because I was convinced – and still am – of their importance, but because I was more interested in literature than in semantics I occasionally tried to steer him away from discussing 'The cat is on the mat'. I seldom succeeded. We agreed that Chekhov was a great dramatist, so why discuss him? Or Shaw? Or Shakespeare? As for Samuel Beckett, Wynburne's rival who beat him into second place in the moderatorship degree examination in modern languages at Trinity, well, for Beckett's literary achievement he had the highest praise, recognising the 'tremendous effort, courage and honesty needed in his search for his identity, his centre, the meaning of existence, the answer to the human predicament'. I quote this sentence from an article (rejected) that Wynburne submitted to a newspaper. What I think I liked most about him was

137

his complete lack of envy. At twenty-one years of age he and Beckett were running neck and neck academically: Beckett ended with a Nobel Prize and worldwide recognition, Wynburne with a privately printed book on the application of Basic English to schools. What both shared was a degree of personal integrity that is rare.

Wynburne wished to donate his body for medical research, but when he died of a heart attack at the age of seventy-seven, his body was of no use to medical science. He would have been sorry: he always used the word 'science' with reverence and tried to serve it in his own way.

His daughters asked me to speak at his cremation at Roselawn. It was a simple service and I remember quoting a sentence from Henry James's beautiful story 'The Middle Years': 'We work in the dark – we do what we can – we give what we have. Our doubt is our passion and our passion is our task.' I do not know whether Stephen admired Henry James, but I think he would have approved of this sentence. I was tempted, but lacked the courage, to tell one of his own favourite stories. A few years before his death Stephen had had a heart attack on his way to his cottage in north Antrim and was taken to the hospital at Ballymena. A young nurse asked him what his religion was and he replied, 'Scientific humanist.'

'Spell it, please,' she said. 'I never heard tell of that one.'

'S-c-i-e-n-t-i-f-i-c h-u-m-a-n-i-s-t,' he replied, beginning to lose consciousness and spelling out the words slowly. Then, at what he thought might well be the moment of death, he heard her voice faintly spelling the words back to him in confirmation. 'S-c-i-e-n-t-i-f-i-c h-u-m-o-r-i-s-t.'

He managed to shake his head in denial before becoming unconscious. Having survived to tell his tale, he cheerfully accepted both definitions of his faith.

By the time I had spent ten years with the BBC in Belfast I was almost certain that I would spend the rest of my professional life there. Frank O'Connor continued to advise me to get out, warning me that sooner or later I would find the atmosphere stifling, that I was bound to become soured with the narrowness of provincial life. But O'Connor loved simplifying his problems and I had no intention of taking his advice. Leaving Ireland might have helped to advance his own career, but we both knew that he became unhappy as soon as he was six months out of the country and longed to be back, preferably in Dublin where he had plenty of enemies – and a few friends – to provoke him into action. He liked America and England and France for short spells, but he was an Irish writer and he loved Ireland. It gave me intense pleasure that I made him feel at home in the North, so much so that he once thought seriously of settling here. Naturally I warned him against it.

O'Connor was a genius, though his particular kind of genius often got him into trouble in Ireland. Sometimes he liked to imagine himself a Protestant, especially when a Catholic bishop or the Pope himself made some pronouncement that roused his anger and caused him to bare his teeth like a wild animal in captivity. What angered him most was the censorship of books, which had made Ireland the laughing stock of every intellectual in the world. O'Connor, Sean O'Faolain and Peadar O'Donnell were in the vanguard of the anti-censorship struggle, particularly during the years of their editorship of *The Bell*. This censorship was a disgraceful episode in Ireland's intellectual history and cannot be forgotten by anyone who lived through it. Some of O'Connor's own work was of course banned, but though, like Shaw, O'Casey and Joyce he appeared to revel in a fight, I do not believe he or they actually did. It is a truism that writers are too absorbed in their own work to enjoy distractions;

although controversy is all very well – and sometimes unavoidable – it gets in the way of their real work, like brambles in a country lane.

O'Connor's whole life was strewn with brambles. He was attracted to women and they were attracted to him. He was handsome, but not at all in any conventional sense, with his prematurely greying hair, high forehead, bushy eyebrows, full lips fronted with a ridiculous Hitleresque moustache, and firm chin; his complexion, except after a cycling holiday, was sallow. He walked with a long, confident stride, his shoulders slightly hunched, his eyes – were they greenish? – peering at passers-by. He never tired of staring at babies in their prams, and of course he could never pass a bookshop. He must have been very familiar with the Dublin bookshops, and he certainly grew to like those in Belfast. Once, walking in Donegall Square, he enjoyed a bonus – a baby parked in front of Erskine Mayne's bookshop. As babies all look more or less alike to me – I can never guess their gender correctly – I left him to communicate with his baby and entered the shop, which interested me much more. About a quarter of an hour passed and there was no sign of him: I began to wonder whether he had stolen the wretched infant. I went out and found him engrossed not only with the baby but with its mother, a good-looking young woman. They were discussing the infant's character and idiosyncracies. I hauled him away by telling him I had found an attractive two-volume edition of Stendhal's *Lucien Leuwen*, which he promptly bought. Then he added, 'I want to buy something for that son of yours you say doesn't like books. I wonder is there anything here.' He found and bought a good edition of *Huckleberry Finn* and handed it over to me. 'Tell Gavin to try that.'

We left the bookshop discussing the iniquities of any school that failed to kindle an enthusiasm for reading in its pupils,

O'Connor disregarded my suggestion that our home was *too* full of books and that Gavin's distaste for books was my fault and not the school's. Deprived almost entirely of formal education himself, O'Connor loved me to talk about mine.

'I'd far too much of it,' I assured him.

'Of the wrong kind,' he replied.

'Yes, of course. I hardly survived it.'

He would have enjoyed a university, or so he imagined; at any rate he missed the cachet of a university degree. So when Trinity College Dublin gave him an honorary doctorate he felt that at last he had arrived and was publicly acknowledged in his own country. Like most people I know who have not had a university education, O'Connor overvalued the experience; likewise I, who would have relished a couple of years at Oxford or the Sorbonne, sometimes feel that I may have missed something of real value. Most of us live our lives with such illusions, but the truth is that finally we are all autodidacts. In my own case, the years I spent at a university were almost useless, except for getting a job at the end. The self-education that Shaw, O'Casey and O'Connor gave themselves was of a different order. Above all, it was joyful.

Nine years older than I was – he was born in 1903 – and when we met in 1946 already for many years a famous writer, O'Connor looked on me – as he looked on everybody – as an equal. He had the gift of friendship, of instantly liking people. It was a dangerous gift, perhaps, but it was in his nature. My own friendship with him was immediate; I think it was forged when he learned that I belonged to the working class not only by origin but by instinctive sympathy and that I had had to struggle for my 'superior' education. He envied me my knowledge of Latin (which was not as great as he imagined) and we commiserated with one another because neither had any Greek (I kept hidden from him that I had learned a little when I was a teacher).

141

It was O'Connor's short stories that I knew best and most admired. The novel *Dutch Interior*, which I had tried to read more than once, struck me as dull, without the vitality of his best stories – I'm thinking of 'Guests of the Nation', 'Uprooted', 'The Long Road to Ummera', 'My Oedipus Complex', 'The Bridal Night', 'First Confession', 'The Majesty of the Law'. O'Connor's greatest stories are oral: they jump off the page, and contain the resonances and the nuances of his own voice. I remember he once asked what I was reading and when I told him *Madame Bovary* his reaction was an unexpected one. 'Are you now? Well, the advantage of reading Flaubert is that you'll find it hard to be a *bad* writer.' His answer puzzled me for a while, because though I could easily grasp the obvious meaning – that at least you will take care of your style and search for *le mot juste* – I suspected he had something else in mind. What this was became clearer as we worked together recording story after story.

When I first began producing O'Connor's stories for radio my method was the conventional one then used by BBC producers. First I would do a 'timing' run-through, the purpose being to find out roughly the story's duration. I would use my stopwatch and at the bottom of each page note the exact duration in minutes and seconds. The times allotted to the stories varied between fifteen minutes and half an hour, but most of O'Connor's stories were twenty minutes – about 3,000 words – or a little longer, depending on the pace required for the story, the proportion of dialogue to narration and so on. O'Connor appeared to be little concerned with *le mot juste*: if the story was too long we would make cuts and time it again.

As we gained experience in working with each other we modified this method of production, having come to the conclusion that the less rehearsal we had, the more spontaneous the telling of the story would be. The principle was that we should

142

sacrifice anything in order to achieve the spontaneity of the seanachie. The so-called producer was almost and, ideally, completely unnecessary, except as the single listener. This became my role, and it was a happy one.

So instead of the normal hour or hour and a half of run-throughs – which we agreed 'killed' the story – we almost dispensed with rehearsals. The two of us would enter the studio only a quarter of an hour before transmission or recording, and merely to enable the engineers to do a 'balance'. O'Connor would read the passage during which his voice would be at its loudest, then the passage at which his voice would be at its lowest, and finally he would read something at his normal volume for narration. And that would be it. End of rehearsal. The most important thing was that I should have complete faith in him to tell his story in the allotted time, but like a musical conductor I would guide and control him to that end by gestures. If I wanted him to increase the pace I would make a circular motion with my right arm, rotating it very slowly if the pace was to be quickened slightly, and increasing the speed if I judged the pace was dragging seriously. If, however, the story was being delivered too fast I would slowly open my arms wide in a gesture of benediction. O'Connor was adamant that he should tell his story only to a single listener, in a one-to-one relationship. If either he or I thought of the tens or hundreds of thousands of listeners there were in reality our illusion would be lost. The story would be a public performance instead of a private, intimate confession.

Spontaneity was all – or, more accurately, the effect of spontaneity was all. O'Connor was not a spontaneous writer like Stendhal or Trollope, two writers he enormously admired; he made draft after draft of many of his stories, revising and revising until he was more or less satisfied. Never entirely, of course: that was the ideal. Only once do I recall him being completely satisfied after reading a story, his long sigh betokening achieved perfection as he lit a cigarette and blew the smoke high into the stale air of the studio.

'Well, how did it go, Jack?' (He had called me by my familiar name ever since he once had heard my wife use it. He did that to signify our close friendship. For the same reason I had begun to call him Michael once I heard his mother call him by his baptismal name.)

'Perfect, Michael,' I said, deeply moved.

'That's the best I've ever done. I hope you've recorded it. I don't think I could ever do as well again.'

The story was one of his finest, the lyrical ballad-like 'The Bridal Night'. O'Connor called it his 'Synge song' in an attempt to cool my ardour for his perfect story; it has a flavour of Synge, of course, but I see no harm in that. When he broadcast 'The Bridal Night' I quizzed him about his early life – he had not then written *An Only Child* but I suspected he might have spent some time in a lonely spot in Ireland far from Cork; he only laughed and said, 'No, I'm a townie, a real townie.' As I have just mentioned *An Only Child*, the first volume of his autobiography, I should add that I regard it as his masterpiece. I also like to imagine, perhaps fondly, that I helped to plant the seed or one of the seeds. O'Connor had come with me to Limavady where I had been recording a discussion programme, and afterwards the writer George Buchanan had invited us to his house for something to eat and drink. It was well after midnight when the two of us left the house, having refused George's offer to bring us back by car to the town. It was a cold, starry night and we linked arms as we walked along the rutted lane from the house to the road. After stumbling into a rut we stopped for a moment to regain our balance and O'Casey's line from *Juno and the Paycock*

144

came into my head: 'An', as it blowed an' blowed, I ofen looked up at the sky an' assed meself the question – what is the stars, what is the stars?' We stood for a while looking up at the night sky, our trousers wet from the puddles in the lane. O'Connor lit a cigarette.

'What do you believe in, Michael?' I asked, warmed by Buchanan's whiskey.

'Something,' he said. 'I don't know what.'

'Inspiration?'

'Yes, a little of that – and hard work.'

'God?'

'Who knows?'

It was chatter on my part, aimed at probing him, but I was unsuccessful in my role of Boswell and we walked along in silence.

'You must write your autobiography, Michael,' I said at last.

'You think I must?'

'For a good reason – I'd like to read it. You've written stories for me, haven't you?'

'Yes,' he said, adding, 'well, maybe, some day.' When the time came he sent me the *New Yorker*, in which episodes of *An Only Child* appeared, and when the book itself was published he handed me a copy with the words, 'Well, there you are. You asked for it, didn't you?'

It is a book I treasure not only for the story it tells of O'Connor's early years of poverty and his struggle for an education but also for the photographs it contains of his mother Minnie O'Connor O'Donovan who, when I first met her, was living with Michael in his roomy house at 57 Strand Road, Sandymount, overlooking Dublin Bay. She asked me to call her Donny because Michael called her that and I was his friend, and it seemed natural to do so. But she always called me 'Mr Boyd' when the two of us were alone, reserving the familiarity of 'Jack' or 'John' for times when Michael was present. She always followed his whim. Because Michael talked about literature to me, Donny also talked about literature to me when Michael was out of the room and we were alone. On one occasion she produced for my benefit an old periodical, tattered but carefully preserved, opened it reverently and pointed to a story. 'That's the first one he ever did,' she said slowly. 'It's the best one he ever wrote. So I think, but he doesn't agree.'

When Michael appeared in the room and noticed the tattered periodical on her lap, he growled, 'What's that oul wan talkin' about?' His air of gruffness was, of course, the cloak he assumed to cover his love.

'I was only talking about your first story –'

'Away upstairs wi' ye,' he growled again, adding to me, 'I've to protect you against that woman. I know she's flirtin' with ye.'

'Don't ever say that, son, because it's not true.'

'Oh, it's the truth, else I wouldn't say it of ye.'

'Michael!'

The truth was the opposite: he was doing all the flirting, and Donny knew it and was pleased and embarrassed at what she considered her son's misbehaviour. So she left the room and went upstairs to her own room.

'I know how to get rid of her,' he said, pleased with himself. It was a game they played and at first I thought it a strange way of showing affection. But as O'Connor admitted, throughout his life he was a mother's boy, the victim of a deep Oedipus complex. It could not have been otherwise, for Donny was saintly in her simplicity and her son worshipped her. To the other women in his life he gave affection, perhaps deep affection, but love was kept for the small, courageous woman brought up in an orphanage, whose life had inspired his own.

I did not know Michael intimately until I had read the early chapters of *An Only Child*, and afterwards I felt no need to delve into his past: it is all there in the book, so poignantly rendered that I find it best not to read more than a few pages at a time. It is impossible to read this autobiography without learning to love O'Connor. Certainly he had a sharp tongue when he felt that somebody had done him down, and from time to time he had personal feuds, especially in Dublin literary circles. Michael expected loyalty from his friends and if he needed sympathy I gave it, in the knowledge that if it failed to bring him serenity it at least diminished his misery. He was a worrier: he worried about his mother, his children, his women, himself; still, he managed most of the time to keep his anxieties to himself. Occasionally, however, this proved impossible. Once, when I was in Dublin unknown to him and not intending to call at Strand Road, I suddenly changed my mind and telephoned him.

'How are you, Michael?'

'Is that you, Jack?'

'Yes. I'm in Dublin. Would you like me to call?'

'No! I'm in rotten form, awful!'

'Then I won't call. See you soon.'

'No, no! Come and see me now! But I'm in rotten form ... '

'Are you sure you want to see me?'

'Yes, yes, come, come along ... Now!'

'I've Louis Johnston with me here. Would you like to see him too?'

'Yes, yes. Come on, the pair of you! At least I can give you a drink. I'll be waiting for you.'

Louis Johnston was a friend of mine from Belfast who had set up his office equipment business in Dublin and whom I had introduced to Michael. Louis spoke French and Spanish well and had impressed Michael with his enthusiasm for Lorca.

Marjory, Louis' wife, was also a good linguist and Michael had taken a liking to both of them.

As soon as Michael opened the door for us it was apparent that something serious was wrong. He had a wild, half-crazed look on his face, his hair was dishevelled and he was in his shirtsleeves. I did not ask him what the matter was for I knew he would soon tell me.

'Here, have a drink,' he said, handing us a half-empty bottle of whiskey and going to the kitchen for glasses. When he returned he said, with venom in his voice, 'Look out there! What d'you see there?'

'Have you had a fire?' Louis asked.

'Yes, a bonfire!

'What for?' Louis asked.

'Getting rid of a load of junk.'

We went into the garden and O'Connor prodded the smouldering fire into life. It was made up of newspapers, magazines and cuttings of articles and stories of his own. Whether the bonfire contained any of his manuscripts I am not certain. All I recall is that when we returned into the room he took a typescript from the table and handed it to me with the words, 'You may as well have that – if you'd like to have it.' It was the typescript of *The Fountain of Magic*, his translations from the Irish, with emendations in pencil by W.B. Yeats. I was reluctant to accept it but thought that the circumstances demanded that I should not refuse. Later I could return it; so when I went back to Louis Johnston's flat I left the typescript in his safe keeping rather than bring it back with me to Belfast. Shortly afterwards Louis returned the valuable typescript to its rightful owner.

This was, I think, the only time I was in O'Connor's company when he was in a highly nervous state of tension. He had plenty of excuse to be. Evelyn, his wife, had just left him after a series of rows and gone to her mother in Wales, bringing the children with her. That night, after Louis and I had departed, O'Connor walked along the shore until midnight, packed his bags and left 57 Strand Road for good. He was again without a home, and departed for London for a few weeks before returning to Dublin to find refuge in Louis and Marjory Johnston's flat, where he could relax in congenial company. And there he remained for some months.

Michael O'Donovan's life turned out to be restless though he never gave me the impression of being a restless man. Yet I suppose he must have been. Curiously enough, on the occasions when we met, and they were many, we were usually going from one place to another, mostly on foot but sometimes in my old Rover car. Luckily Michael took no interest in cars as such, looking on them merely as a convenient method of transport not to be preferred to a good bicycle or his own two legs. Still, the car did give us an opportunity to talk about literature uninterrupted for hours on end, for I was a slow driver and we were never in a hurry to reach our destination.

We usually went for trips in the North to see old churches, castles or houses, which gave him a chance to display his knowledge of architecture, a chance he never missed. Sometimes we left Belfast to spend the afternoon in places like Bangor, Newtownards, Lisburn, Greyabbey, Downpatrick, always in search of what was old, and the older the better. Once we shared a magical moment when we stopped in our tracks a few yards outside the Cistercian Abbey at Greyabbey. Michael suddenly held my arm and whispered, 'Listen.' We stood still. From somewhere near at hand we could hear a boys' choir singing. 'Palestrina,' Michael said. We stood until the voices ceased before proceeding to the abbey itself just in time to see the schoolboys and their teacher disperse. The moment had passed. The choir singing

149

Palestrina had been transformed into a noisy group of school-boys eager to escape from the tutelage of their teacher. The little incident moved both O'Connor and me, O'Connor who declared himself an agnostic though I am not certain he was, and me who, if not born an agnostic, had become one while still at school. O'Connor may have lost the orthodoxy of his Catholic faith when a young man, but as an old man the beauty of the ritual and the glory of medieval churches gave him delight.

Another little incident, almost farcical, occurred when we went to Hillsborough, a village which O'Connor thought one of the most beautiful in Ireland. He was very eager to see the Governor's residence and disappointed when I told him that entry to the house and grounds was not permitted. Nevertheless, for confirmation we approached the policeman on sentry duty at the main gates.

'I'm sorry, sir, but this is as far as you can get,' he said.

'But my friend here,' I pleaded, 'is a distinguished scholar, with a particular interest in architecture. He would like to view the house from the front.'

'Sorry, sir, but'd be against orders. If the Governor wasn't in residence I might be able to let you both slip inside for a couple of minutes. But he's here at present and you might run into him. And then – '

'I understand,' Michael said in his most conciliatory tone of voice, before turning away. 'Thank you very much.'

'Where d'you come from, sir?' the policeman asked.

'Cork.'

'I thought you were from the other side of the border. You're hardly a member of the IRA, are you?'

'No, not now,' Michael replied. 'But I once was.'

The policeman gave a hearty laugh and turned to me. 'I think I know you, sir. Mr Boyd, isn't it?'

I admitted to the name.

'You don't remember me, sir, but I remember you.'

'Oh, when and where did we meet?'

'At school, sir. You taught me English and history at Lisburn Intermediate.' He gave me his name and I remembered it but not the face. So we shook hands and I introduced him to Michael, explaining that this person from Cork was a well-known Irish writer who frequently broadcast his stories on the BBC.

'I knew you were only taking a hand out of me, sir, tellin' me you were in the IRA.'

'I was,' Michael reiterated, 'but a couple of years in prison knocked all that nonsense out of me!'

'I'd like to believe you, sir, but if you ask me you're a bit of a liar.'

My ex-pupil, a big sandy-haired fellow from Lisburn, gave his cackle of a laugh, and Michael commented, 'You could be right. I'm a professional liar.'

'Aye, I'd believe that.'

We turned away from the main gates but my ex-pupil called us back. 'Ach, slip on past me when I'm not lookin'. But mind an' stay in the front garden, else you'll have me court-martialled.' Then he said to me, 'You haven't changed a bit, sir, since the time you used to take us for rugby on the back field.'

Michael had his look at the Governor's residence. I remember we had a glimpse of the Governor and his wife strolling across the lawns. They each acknowledged our presence with a wave of the hand, and we acknowledged theirs similarly. And so everyone was satisfied.

Like all writers, O'Connor liked praise for his work, and I gave him plenty of that. I thought him the best writer of short stories in the English language and told him so. But he would not agree and nominated Hemingway. I suppose I was biased in

151

O'Connor's favour, especially as I had heard he held a high opinion of my critical judgement. Once, after he had recorded a story, he asked me how it had sounded and I shook my head. 'No, not so good,' I said. My adverse comment surprised him but all he remarked was, 'A pity. It's the best I can do. Let's go somewhere for a drink.' Over a drink I confessed to him that I thought that the story itself was not one of his best and that maybe I should not have accepted it. 'No, you shouldn't have,' he answered vehemently. 'You ought to have rejected it and I could have given you another one.' He was highly self-critical, sometimes rewriting a story more than twenty times in an attempt to get it right; at other times, his first version satisfied him, but this I think was rare.

The main reason for the solidity of our friendship may have been that we met only about four times every year, in Belfast, in Dublin or in London, and only for a couple of days on each occasion. Usually I arranged some broadcasting: an interview, a book review, a story or a talk on some theme such as the Cuchulain Cycle. Probably our happiest meetings took place in Belfast, where he was able to relax, and forget, momentarily at least, his entanglements of one sort or another and chat to people like Joe Tomelty, Roy McFadden, Sam Bell and others.

Two broadcasts I remember vividly. One was a discussion between O'Connor and Denis Johnston on the problem of Swift's relationship to Stella. This was an unrehearsed, unscripted affair, and the two speakers had a dingdong battle about the complexities of Swift's character, each convinced that the other was talking nonsense. I thought that Johnston got the better of the argument, mainly because he knew more about Swift than O'Connor did, and his rapierlike, legalistic method of argument proved more effective than O'Connor's bludgeoning dogmatism. It was a contest between a disciplined mind and a comparatively undisciplined one. Never before had I heard two superb broadcasters in full-blooded debate, sometimes snarling and sneering at each other across the studio table, with the phallus-shaped microphone separating them like some silent deity. The second broadcast was again a dialogue, the subject being Irish drama, O'Connor's opponent was Tyrone Guthrie. Here the roles were reversed: O'Connor could speak with more authority than Guthrie about Irish drama in its particularities, but Guthrie could properly assume a knowledge of dramatic principles and practice which was denied his opponent. The discussion ran on smooth lines, both speakers conceding points gracefully and with great good humour.

I got special pleasure from initiating and producing these two discussions by men whose friendship I enjoyed and valued. All three were dramatists, Denis Johnston being the most distinguished, indeed after Sean O'Casey's death in 1964, I considered him to be the best living Irish dramatist. Johnston and O'Casey had never got on well together, for both were outspoken and abrasive. Still, Johnston seldom failed to pay tribute to O'Casey's genius and was sometimes fulsome in his praise: for instance, when writing about his own play *The Scythe and the Sunset*, which deals with the Easter Rebellion of 1916, Johnston discourages any comparison with O'Casey's masterpiece *The Plough and the Stars*, saying that it would be 'the act of an idiot' to compare the two plays. Yet though *The Plough and the Stars* is rightly regarded as one of the greatest plays of the twentieth century, *The Scythe and the Sunset* is far from being a negligible work. It is undervalued and neglected, there is little doubt about that, just as Johnston himself is an undervalued and neglected writer. But I cannot believe that this will always be so.

Johnston himself was a witty, generous and compassionate man with a wide experience of life. He was a lawyer, playwright,

153

autobiographer, metaphysician (alas), journalist, war correspondent, academic, broadcaster, authority on Swift, director of plays – a list which suggests that he may have dissipated his considerable energies. He spent too much of his time outside Ireland and when I once boldly told him so – for his subjects were Irish and his primary interest appeared to be his native country – he barked back, 'I spend much more of my time here than you appear to imagine. At least six months every year.' He admitted all the same that half a year away from Dublin prevented him from being in the swim, that people did not know when he was at home and that he got left out of all sorts of things. In short, he was neglected, assumed to be teaching in some American university while all the time he was sitting in his library at home. Whenever I learned he was at home in Ireland I invited him to Belfast to broadcast, for I knew he liked the city, having worked as a features writer in the BBC before the Second World War.

Many years later, after I had retired from the BBC, I contributed an essay 'The Endless Search' to a volume called *Denis Johnston: a retrospective*, which was published to mark his eightieth birthday. I spent some months writing it and rereading the plays, but when I had finished I felt dissatisfied with the result. The title at least was appropriate: throughout his long life – he died at the age of eighty-five – Denis was a man in pursuit of some philosophy that would reveal to him the meaning of life. He searched endlessly for such a philosophy, but I think failed to find one. Probably his failure was inevitable: few imaginative writers have a talent for abstract thinking. And I find Johnston's attempts at philosophising are wholly implausible. All I can add is that I share Vivian Mercier's judgement that Johnston's final testament, *The Brazen Horn*, was a waste of valuable creative energy.

In *Out of My Class* I have told the story of my first meeting with

154

Denis Johnston when I was a young schoolmaster teaching in a small school in Newry. This was before the Second World War and Denis was then an energetic figure with jet-black hair and a voice that detonated like automatic rifle fire. The last time we met was in 1983, shortly before his death, when his hair had turned white and his walk was slow and uncertain. He had arrived in Belfast for the first night in the Lyric Theatre of *Indian Summer* by his daughter Jennifer. His presence on this occasion was an act of courage, though Denis himself would not have perceived it as such. We had only a few words together as he made his way with difficulty upstairs into the auditorium, his great shaggy head bowed, his breathing hoarse and his speech low. We shook hands and he smiled his farewell.

8

After about ten years in the BBC I grew restless and wanted to return to academic life: not to school teaching but to a post in a university, preferably in the extramural department. I applied for a couple of jobs, got one unsuccessful interview and then concluded that I would have to stay in broadcasting. It was no great hardship to do so. I had learned my craft as a producer in radio and was looking forward to mastering the new craft of television production. However, I was given no encouragement to do so and was told that I was too valuable in my own post. Apparently it did not pay to be considered efficient. Another explanation offered me was that I was too individualistic. That suggestion amused me. I think it meant I was not a yes-man. Certainly I did like getting my own way, was convinced it was the right way, even when those in the BBC hierarchy suggested otherwise. I worked best with writers – that is why I have written about them so much here – and a number of my regional literary programmes were given repeats on the Third Programme which was the most prestigious BBC channel.

MacNeice, Rodgers, Reggie Smith, Jack Dillon, and Rayner Heppenstall were the London producers I envied most, producing programmes like MacNeice's 'The Dark Tower' and Rodgers's collages of Yeats and Joyce. Yet I still made no effort to be transferred to London. I felt I belonged to Belfast even if Belfast did not belong to people like me. My Protestantism was only nominal, Catholicism was alien to me, I had nothing but contempt for everything that unionism as a political creed stood for, and nationalism seemed to me ingrowing, outworn and narrow. And I had no time for individualism, whatever form it might take. I thought of myself as an emotional and scientific socialist debarred from taking an active part in politics by the nature of my work. But my intellectual quest was still in progress. I read widely, wrote little and got a great deal of satisfaction out of my life.

The root of any dissatisfaction I experienced was the fact that I was tied to radio and unable to free myself from it. Like an incubus, it obsessed me. Almost everyone I met I thought of as a potential broadcaster. What programme could I fit him or her into?

I remember once going into a second-hand book-and-furniture shop at the Lisburn Road end of Sandy Row, which was run by a pleasant middle-aged man with a ready smile who always greeted me warmly, though I often left without buying a book or an article of furniture. On this occasion he showed me a whole shelf of books. 'These might interest you, sir,' he said, adding, 'they're going very cheap.' They were about thirty volumes of Balzac's *The Human Comedy* with an introduction by George Saintsbury. I bought the lot for about £4. My ambition was, I suppose, to immerse myself in Balzac's great *oeuvre*, whether in English or in French, and to acquaint myself with that unique panorama of human life. I had read only half a dozen of his novels, visited his little house in a Paris suburb, and stood in admiration of Rodin's *Balzac* in the Luxembourg Gardens. And the Christmas before, Joe Tomelty had given me a present of Stefan Zweig's biography of Balzac.

I find it strange that Joe was the person who rekindled my interest in Balzac, for I do not recall ever discussing any French novel with him, but he knew of my interest in French literature – I was given to parading it to my close friends – and he must have gone to some trouble to find this biography. Joe liked books and was very conscious of his lack of formal education. He had spent his boyhood in Portaferry, left school early, became an apprentice to the painting trade and, after he came to Belfast to live, drifted into the theatre. An untrained, natural actor, he turned professional when the Group Theatre was formed, and when I first met him he scraped some kind of a living by combining his acting with looking after the box office. His talent for stage-acting led to radio work, which must have brought him badly needed income. As he wrote short stories and read them himself, I came to know him well. He also wrote radio plays, some of them excellent, which I thought were better than his stories. Then, with his soap opera (the term was not then current) called 'The McCooeys', Joe achieved at least local fame. He may not have made a fortune but at least he received a steady income from this source alone.

Sam Bell and I were responsible for the BBC's selection of Joe to write 'The McCooeys'. Harry McMullan was of the opinion that listeners would prefer a middle-class milieu for the suggested programme: Bell and I insisted that the series should be set in the working class and that Tomelty was the man to write it. Our advice was taken, Joe was offered and accepted the job, and 'The McCooeys' almost at once became the most popular radio programme ever broadcast by this region. Joe not only wrote it but acted in it. Thousands of families stayed at home in order to hear the latest episode; Joe's photograph was constantly in the newspapers and heads were turned in the streets of Belfast when he went for a stroll in the streets, sometimes in the company of Sam Bell and myself. Fame was sweet.

I now believe that by urging the BBC to accept Tomelty as a soap-opera writer we did him a disservice. Popularity pays in the market place, but the price for selling a talent can be too high. Joe Tomelty is still remembered as the author of 'The McCooeys', but his best work – notably his play *All Souls Night* in drama and *The Apprentice*, his second novel – suggests what his potentialities were. In 1957 Joe received severe head injuries in a car accident in England, and was unconscious for many weeks, but almost miraculously he survived. He had been on the brink of stardom both on stage and in films, but his acting career proved to be finished; his writing career too was impaired, and so seriously that it looked unlikely that he would ever again be able to write anything. Though he made great efforts, he failed. He handed me one of his attempts – a short story – about a year and a half after his accident. Psychologically at a low ebb, he needed an injection of encouragement. Though I thought the story not up to standard I urged that it should be broadcast in one of the afternoon slots, when listening figures would be at a minimum. My argument was a moral one: Tomelty had served the BBC well and deserved to be given a chance to rehabilitate himself. The counter-argument was to the effect that if his story was not up to standard, it should be rejected. So I had to write a letter of rejection.

I found this task distasteful, though as an editor writing letters of rejection was one of my duties, which normally I did without qualms of conscience. In this instance, though, I believe I was wrong to accept my superior's decision without protesting much more strongly than I in fact did. Tomelty suffered from this rebuff, and his recovery may have been affected; but so-called standards were maintained, and all was well as far as the Corporation was concerned.

But all was not well with me. I felt – rightly or wrongly – guilty of betraying a friend, of being a Corporation man instead of being myself. And years passed before I regained Tomelty's friendship. During those years Joe has struggled hard to restore himself to his former physical and mental strength, but his memory became too erratic and his movements too uncertain for him to reproduce his former acting ability, and his writing – for he has made attempt after attempt – lacked the vitality characteristic of his talent. When an artist has matured his talent and then is suddenly robbed of it, his adjustment to living requires an heroic effort, an effort which Joe never ceased to make.

My work brought me into closer touch with writers than with other artists, though I became friendly with painters such as Colin Middleton, Tom Carr, George Campbell, Terry Flanaghan, Gerard Dillon, Dan O'Neill, Markey Robinson, Willie Conor, and George MacCann and his wife Mercy. I jot down their names haphazardly because I do not intend to write about them or their work, but the thought strikes me that many of the painters I have known have been able to cocoon themselves by the nature of their art in a way rarely possible to writers, particularly dramatists. A painter's life is a hard and sometimes a lonely one, bringing isolation and often little money, and I believe that I admire painters more than I do writers. But what I envy most of all is their self-sufficiency. Their basic tools are simple. A writer's tools only *appear* to be simpler: pen and paper as against paints and canvases. I am thinking of the organisation and the interference that a writer has to be involved with before a play is experienced on the stage or on radio or television, or before a story is seen in print.

In those restless years of my middle age and mid-career, I forwarded the careers of many writers by producing their work, not only established writers like Frank O'Connor, Sean O'Faolain and Michael McLaverty but also younger writers like Brian Friel, John O'Connor, Mary Beckett and many more. I revelled in my job but more and more felt that I did not want to devote my entire life to interpreting and judging other writers' work. So to satisfy the creative itch I now turned to radio and wrote a few plays, adaptations and documentaries; it was work that gave me some satisfaction and some extra money; though what motivated me was not extra money but a great urge to create something worthwhile.

I reached the conclusion, however, that I could not serve two masters – the BBC *and* literature. Though I was drawn to the theatre I could see no possibility of getting a play of my own accepted by the Group. So I adapted St John Ervine's novel *Mrs Martin's Man*. The director and actor Harold Goldblatt immediately accepted it, it was fairly successful and I learned a good deal about writing for the stage. It was a kind of breakthrough, but it was hardly an achievement to be proud of: essentially hack work. To write an adaptation takes only a few weeks; to write a novel takes months, if not years. My ambition was still to write a long novel of Balzacian proportions, though in sane moments I knew perfectly well that such an effort was out of the question, a pipe dream, and I would find excuses for not attempting it.

Though I had to spend most of my working hours in Broadcasting House producing live and recorded programmes, I often managed to escape. On one occasion Bertie Rodgers made use of me as his *alter ego*. For some reason he was unable to travel to Dublin to interview Richard Best about his memories of James Joyce and I agreed to take his place. After Best – a tall, thin, polite man – had recorded his piece in the Radio Éireann studio at the side of the General Post Office, he and I went for coffee and more gossip (but this time without a microphone to contend with). For me it was like stepping into *Ulysses*, with Stephen Dedalus discussing Goethe and Mallarmé, Shakespeare and Wilde with the Quaker librarian, then 'tall, young, mild light' and still tall, no longer young, but still mild and light. Joyce's adjectives were, as always, *les mots justes*. Best and I spent half an hour over our coffee and he talked away as if he had not had a chance of talking to anyone about Joyce for years. No, he told me, he had not read *Ulysses* but he had heard that it was an awful book and that Joyce had made him one of the characters in it: not a very flattering character either. Joyce had portrayed him as mean because of his refusal to lend Joyce a pound, when the truth was that he only had ten shillings in his pocket. He was not well off at that time. Then he talked to me about his wife and some letters she had written … But I was not in the least interested in Mrs Best's letters and Best had clearly exhausted his interest in Joyce. So we shook hands and he murmured some mild words about Mr Rodgers's health and welfare before disappearing along O'Connell Street. I suppose that that meeting with Best was for me a kind of Joycean epiphany, a memorable moment, but now it is too imprecise and I have to turn to *Ulysses* itself to catch the flavour of the young Quaker expounding literature to the young Stephen Dedalus.

During the fifties and sixties I often had to leave Broadcasting House to work on outside broadcasts, the most memorable perhaps being a popular discussion called 'Your Questions'. I was not keen on producing this programme at first, the main reason being that I disliked appearing in front of audiences to make short, polite speeches of welcome, of explanation of the aims of the programme, and finally of thanks.

The laudable aim of the programme was to bring free speech – or an approximation of free speech – into tens of thousands of homes where such an experience was novel or unknown. Protestants mostly read Protestant newspapers, heard Protestant sermons, and belonged to Protestant clubs and societies. Catholics likewise. It was as if two tribes who shared the same territory – a disputed territory – profoundly distrusted each other because their religious beliefs were different – how different was a matter of dispute; their educational systems were also different – how different was again a matter of dispute; and, to compound their differences, each tribe spoke the same language but with different nuances. English was the common language, but on the lips of Catholics an ancient, long-surviving, almost dead language – Irish – seemed mutely present or miraculously resurrected. Yet the two tribes who seemed to have little in common and looked the same had in reality a great deal in common: friendliness and good neighbourliness; even inter-marriage was frequent. And indissolubly the two tribes were locked together.

The aim of this discussion programme was to increase the area of mutual understanding. The chairman was Desmond G. Neill, a lecturer at Queen's, and a Quaker by religious conviction, who possessed a gently authoritarian manner, was well experienced in debates, and was blessed too with a sense of humour. The four speakers chosen for the initial programme at the beginning of 1954 were John E. Sayers, J.J. Campbell, J.C. Beckett and Charles Brett. All were friends of mine, all were excellent debaters, and all had respect for one another's political views. Sayers was a unionist, Campbell a nationalist, Beckett was non-political in any party sense, and Brett was a member of the Northern Ireland Labour Party. From the beginning they set the civilised tone of this programme and the BBC owes all of them a debt of gratitude. They often reappeared during the long run of the programme, 150 editions first in radio and later on television, and became known as personalities – a label each would have lightly rejected.

Of course I had known Jim Beckett ever since our schooldays at Inst, later as a history teacher at the Royal Academy, and during the Second World War as an occasional visitor to our first home in Ballymacash. I liked him but was never his intimate friend. I was interested in Irish history and had taught it at school level, but Jim was a scholar who had devoted his life to his discipline. The rigour and exactitude necessary for historical scholarship was something I could envy but not emulate. I lacked the patience required and my imagination would insist on breaking in. As a young man Beckett had the reputation of being a misogynist: I was told that in his university classes he preferred the girls to sit at the back rather than at the front of the room, which was contrary to the usual situation of boys sitting as far away as possible from the surveillance of the lecturer and girls, being more eager for knowledge, congregating towards the front. But with maturity Jim seemed much more at ease with the opposite sex. He was a bachelor, like two other historians of my acquaintance, R.B. McDowell of Trinity College Dublin and Louis Lord, who became headmaster of the Royal Academy. The study of history can be a lonely pursuit and as marriage and bringing up a family can be distracting and time-consuming, I am never surprised to learn that a first-class historian prefers a life of loneliness to the gregariousness imposed by matrimony. Bachelordom often leads to the making of an eccentric, and this was the usual tag applied to McDowell with his delivery that sometimes consisted of long sentences more appropriate to the pages of Gibbon or Macauley. R.B. was also noted for the length of his scarf which he wound round and round his neck for warmth and comfort, even in warm weather; I think he once told

164

me that this extraordinary scarf had been knitted by his mother. Clearly he was devoted to it. I remember once at a meeting of historians in Broadcasting House to make arrangements for the publication of *Ulster since 1800* (edited by T.W. Moody and J.C. Beckett) McDowell turned up late in his overcoat and scarf, sweating profusely and pouring forth his apologies, 'I'm sorry, Mr Boyd, very sorry, something happened to me on my way here.' He always referred to me formally as if we had just met for the first time, though he had known me since our schooldays at Inst. I wondered what untoward event had impeded his course from the Great Northern railway station where he had landed off the train from Dublin. 'I was just out of the station when I saw a fire brigade coming down the street, then another one and another one, so I ran after them up towards Sandy Row, I've never been able to resist a fire … But I lost them and had to run back here for this meeting. Fortunate I lost them, wasn't it? Has the meeting long started?'

Charles Brett was studying history at Oxford when I first met him, a tall, sharp-featured, long-haired undergraduate with a pronounced English public school accent. We met in a pub in Oxford when I was in the company of Bill McAlpine and Dylan Thomas. Charles must have overheard my Belfast accent because over a drink he told me that he also came from Belfast and hoped to return there within the next year or so. I asked him to get in touch with me when he did so. When we next met he was a solicitor in his father's office in Chichester Street and had joined the Northern Ireland Labour Party. He was like an exotic bird that had strayed into the wrong nest: an upper-middle-class stray that was bound some day to seek and find another resting place. Undoubtedly an asset to the party, Charles was particularly useful as a spokesman and as a lawyer. An excellent broadcaster with the ability to demolish an opponent's argument, he served his party well during his years of office on the executive and as chairman. He was of course regarded by the unionists as a formidable foe and a traitor to his class, but the hatred he roused in such quarters merely caused him amusement. He never discussed his religious views but I imagine he was an agnostic.

J.J. Campbell was a nationalist and a Catholic whom I had known from my pre-BBC days. Dark-haired, voluble, humorous, he never paraded his classical scholarship nor his knowledge of Irish mythology. He was a lecturer in a Catholic training college and later became Professor of Education at Queen's, promotion that his friends thought well deserved and others regarded as proof of his careerism. For a liberal Catholic like Campbell to be promoted to a university chair was something I thoroughly approved of and the whispered allegations struck me as sour grapes.

Jack Sayers was more remote than Campbell, Brett or Beckett but he got on well with all three, even though their political views were fundamentally opposed to his. None was a professional politician in the sense that their replies to controversial questions had to coincide with the party line, and I found their replies refreshingly individual when compared to the stereotyped answers boringly trotted out by members of either the Stormont or Westminster parliaments. Perhaps an exception was Harford Hyde who, though an indifferent performer with a hesitant manner, had an independent mind. Like Beckett and Brett, Hyde was an historian with an interest in literature; if only he had been a livelier speaker he would have been in the 'Your Questions' team more often.

For about a decade this programme was central to my work. It involved journeys to almost every town and village in Northern Ireland, occasionally by train but often by taxi. I had to do what were called 'reconnaissances' beforehand to find out what living in each town was like, the religious and political divisions, the halls where all sorts of people gathered together socially, the ones which were strictly for 'their own sort', who the most influential opinion-formers were, the relationships of the various clergy, the general social atmosphere of the town. Arranging the progamme bore some resemblance to a military operation, with the British invaders venturing into unknown Irish territory on the far side of Lough Neagh into the Sperrin Mountains, or southwards to counties Armagh and Fermanagh, but stopping short of the border dividing the North from the Republic. Sometimes the halls were only half full, sometimes packed, and the audiences were usually a mixture of Protestants and Catholics in more or less the right proportions, and with Catholic and Protestant representatives facing the microphones. With admission free, and with the occasional baby in arms and a stray dog or two included in the audience, I think that, on the whole, a good evening was had by all. There were occasional rows, not much petulance, a good deal of humour, some political crossfire, and a general air of tolerance. Technically the BBC engineers made it an extraordinarily smooth and efficient operation.

'Your Questions' was regarded as an influential regional programme in its time, but it is now forgotten, like even better programmes, for radio is an ephemeral medium, and those who devote their lives to it find themselves at the end without a legacy. Even the most talented BBC writer I knew – Louis MacNeice – may have dissipated his rare gift for writing poetry, having been wooed away from the discipline of his true art. He needed a job, of course, and being a writer-producer on the BBC staff is an attractive job; but I cannot think it a job for a man whose primary ambition was – or should have been – to be one of the greatest poets of the twentieth century.

The political part of my work as producer I had little stomach for, simply because local politics seemed to me so perverted and debased by the politicians (including some of those I had to work with) that I began to see myself as a kind of puppet master. My responsibility was to keep a proper 'balance' in these discussions so that the various parties should be properly represented, and I took this responsibility very seriously indeed, weighing the ability of one speaker against the other so that the programme would not turn into a political broadcast for one party. I have no intention here of discussing the merits and demerits of politicians such as Brian Faulkner, William Craig, Bill Henderson, David Bleakley, Vivian Simpson, Harry Diamond, Irene Calvert, Maurice May, Patricia McLaughlin, J.G. Lennon, Phelim O'Neill, Brian McConnell, Charles Stewart and many others. They are now dead or forgotten, their political course run. They had their day and it is now over, with many of the problems they faced or pretended to face still unsolved – unemployment, bad housing, sectarianism and the rest.

I always turned with relief to broadcasting programmes about the arts. To arrange a review of a good book or play or painting exhibition gave me great pleasure. To be responsible, as producer, for a series of snip-snap discussions on serious social issues by politicians who thought in clichés gave me great pain. I had a feeling of having joined a cabal for the blanketing of clear thought. It was also a relief when on some pretext I had the chance to leave Belfast for three or four days to attend meetings or record programmes in London.

My closest friend in London was Bill Naughton, who lived in a ground-floor flat at 64 St George's Square, a short distance from Victoria Station. I got to know Bill through Frank O'Connor, who invited us both to a Greek restaurant in Soho.

'I want you to meet Bill,' O'Connor had said. 'I know you'll like him. He's Irish. Comes from Mayo and his face reminds me of the map of Ireland, but his accent is English. He was brought up in Bolton, of all places.'

O'Connor was right. Naughton was as Irish-looking as any Irish navvy on a London building site, with his large head, muscular build, jaunty step, outdoor complexion, fleshy nose, loud laugh, twinkling blue eyes and irresistible sense of humour. That evening he invited me to stay at his flat as I had made no arrangements to stay at an hotel. It proved to be the beginning of a long friendship.

Staying with Naughton gave me insight into what it was like to be a struggling middle-aged, working-class writer in London. Bill's sparsely furnished but comfortable flat had a large living room, where he slept, and a smaller kitchen, where he had an iron single bed which suited me very well. The lavatory was along the hallway and the bathroom (Bill took a cold bath every morning) was on the first floor. For me this flat proved to be the best place in London to spend a day or a week.

At that time Bill was scraping a living by writing short stories and an occasional radio play. It was a precarious life, very different from the coalbagging and lorry driving he had done as a younger man, but if it was precarious he never appeared to let that worry him as long as he was able to pay the rent (which was small because he had found the flat during the Blitz) and had enough money for his simple meals and a little over to buy writing paper. It may have been a spartan life but it did not appear so. Bill generated happiness wherever he went. He taught me a good deal about living in London – the joy of playing football in Hyde Park, of spending an hour at the National Gallery or in Soho, of walking by the Thames towards Battersea power station or towards the Tate Gallery where we once spotted Bertrand Russell gazing from his flat at the river traffic.

Bill's flat was a rendezvous for Irishmen eager for good talk, a cup of tea and sandwiches, and sometimes a bottle of wine. O'Connor was a frequent visitor and loved to expound his theories of what constitutes a good short story. Whenever he chanced to read one of Bill's stories in some magazine or paper he would praise it to begin with, then pick out what he considered its faults. I remember one day when O'Connor was shaving in the kitchen, lathering his cheeks and chin with gusto as he dogmatised on the principles that should never be flouted by any storyteller.

'The trouble with that story of yours, Bill, is this!' He paused and began to flourish his razor, pulling his face into contortions, and baring his teeth to give emphasis to his words. 'It lacks organic form.'

'Organic form?' Bill repeated from his chair at the table in the living room, winking at me. 'What the hell is that? How'll I know when my story has it if I don't know what it is?'

'You know perfectly well what organic form is. But if you don't you shouldn't be writing short stories.'

'Shouldn't I?'

'No, you should not.'

'What then should I be writing?'

'You shouldn't be writing at all.'

'What would you advise me to do.'

'Go back to the lorry driving.'

By this time Bill had had enough of O'Connor's pontification. 'You don't know what you're talkin' about, Michael! That's all show-off stuff you heard from some professor! Why the hell should I worry about your organic form or whatever it is when I'm trying to get truth into my story. That's what I'm after – truth! Truth! No faking! I suppose Somerset Maugham has organic form. He's that kind of faker, isn't he?'

I thought that O'Connor was in danger of slitting his own throat as he swathed his cheeks and chin, staring short-sightedly in the direction of Naughton and looking as if he would gladly slit Naughton's throat, given a chance to do so. But all was well. O'Connor had made a few nicks to his chin and put on his glasses to see the self-inflicted damage, and Naughton got up from his chair and stood at the mantelpiece in front of the unlit fire, grinning.

During the fifties and sixties I made many trips to London on BBC business, but having recorded the two or three programmes that occasioned the visit and spent an hour or so in the pubs near Broadcasting House I usually cut loose on my own to do exactly what I wanted – wander round Soho, drop into a Lyons Corner House for a cup of tea and a bun, explore the bookshops along Charing Cross Road, drop into a cinema and, best of all, go to a theatre. In Belfast I felt starved of theatre, and on my first visits to London I glutted myself with fashionable plays whose names I have forgotten. Nevertheless I was fortunate enough to see Olivier in *Oedipus*, *The Entertainer* and *The Dance of Death*. Most memorable of all, however, were the visits of the Berliner Ensemble and especially the first night of *Mutter Courage*.

But without Naughton's friendship I would have felt lonely, for the chatter in the pubs round Broadcasting House bored me. MacNeice and Rodgers were quiet when sober, and tedious when drunk. Curiously I enjoyed their company only when they were in Belfast, drunk or sober, especially when they were with George and Mercy MacCann or in the Elbow Room. In London people passed me by as if I were a shadow, and I felt homeless without Elizabeth and the children, but once arrived there I was almost bound to have an adventure of one kind or another. I remember meeting Louis Johnston somewhere in London, introducing him to Naughton and spending the evening at the flat

171

in St George's Square. It was an ordinary convivial evening of talk and wine, at the end of which I had promised Louis that I would accompany him to Paris on the following morning. Louis took every possible chance to arrange business trips to France, not because he had business to do there, but simply because he had a passion for speaking the French language, which he did with fluency. He combined this accomplishment with the composition of lyrical verse which he loved to recite to his friends in his sonorous voice in expectation of their approval. He made friends easily, and immediately we arrived at our Paris hotel he began chatting to a young couple in French, but he found they were from Birmingham and had never been out of England before. Their ignorance of France amazed him and he soon turned it to his advantage. Harry and Doris were in their thirties and their visit to Paris was intended to be their pre-honeymoon trip, but knowing no French they felt ill at ease and had made up their minds to return to England after only one night in Paris instead of a week. As they had a car Louis at once took them under his wing and persuaded them to venture southwards rather than return to England. He promised to act as their guide and chauffeur for the pleasure of their company and a lift in their car for himself and myself. They agreed. Two days later we had reached Cannes (Louis having driven most of the way), then with handshakes and an exchange of addresses we agreed to part. Louis had taught them a few words of French and booked them into a single room at Bourges, assuring the apparently reluctant Doris that for an engaged couple this was the custom of the country. He convinced himself that he had made their pre-honeymoon trip a success and that they would find their way back to Birmingham without too much trouble.

After three days on the Riviera Louis and I returned to London, he to transact some business there and I to explain that

I had taken a few days' leave in lieu of overtime. I had bathed in the Mediterranean for the first time in my life. Some weeks later Louis received a letter from Doris telling him that she and Harry had arrived home safely and would soon be taking a proper honeymoon but that they had decided on Cornwall rather than France.

The reason for my recalling this madcap escapade is to highlight a streak of waywardness and irresponsibility which someone like Louis could induce me to share with him. He was a short, bulky, Falstaffian figure whose almost circular, moon-like face was for years disfigured by a partial paralysis that gave him the appearance of a clown. His wife Marjory was in most respects his opposite: petite, quiet, subdued. She shared his love of French and accepted his many friends with tolerance and generosity. Frank O'Connor was grateful to both of them after his break-up with Evelyn, when he was left homeless and found refuge in their Dublin flat. But Louis's friendships had a habit of ending abruptly, and some incident happened that soured O'Connor's former affection for him. I never met Louis after his brief intervention into O'Connor's life, but I was saddened to hear of his death many years later. He died, appropriately enough, in Le Havre, on one of his many visits to his beloved France.

My own friendship with O'Connor lasted until his death in 1966. Other people knew him more intimately and saw him more often, but because we saw each other only infrequently we came fresh for news and gossip every time we met, whether in Belfast, Dublin or London, whether alone (which I enjoyed most of all because then he was always relaxed) or in the company of Denis Johnston or Tyrone Guthrie, or in the company of some of the women in his life – Evelyn, Joan or Harriet. I liked all three but knew Harriet best, and when she married him and the three

173

of us were together her American youthful high spirits were infectious, and his deep affection and love for her, and hers for him, were undeniable.

That O'Connor was one of the greatest Irishmen of his time I have no doubt. Ireland made him and mauled him about so much that his genius – even his sanity – was imperilled. Being an intensely vulnerable human being he was not without faults, but his frailties recede into insignificance when viewed against the many obstacles he had to overcome throughout his life. He was a formidable foe and when he met philistinism he blasted it venomously, rejoicing in the strength of his verbal armoury. Sometimes indeed he enjoyed, or seemed to enjoy, his personal feuds; sometimes I thought it would have been better for his own peace of mind to have ignored some of the Dublin littérateurs who got under his skin. Whenever our talk turned to their doings and sayings I became bored and switched off my attention: and he usually perceived my eagerness to exchange opinions with him on more important subjects.

He was always interested in young or not-so-young writers struggling to make their way into literature. In 1958, when he was living in New York, I had a letter from him. Here's part of it.

My dear Jack,

I've just had one of those experiences from which we writers pray to be delivered, a parcel containing stories written in pencil on old school copy books which reached me from somebody called Miss Isobel McColl, 16 Knocklofty Park, Belfast. At the same time I dread even more ignoring poor people like that, and I glanced through them. I have written to her suggesting she send some of them to you. They seem to me on a first reading the Belfast equivalent of Grandma Moses, a complete natural, but with absolutely genuine talent, and with beautiful feeling. The style is extraordinary, a mixture of semi-literate council school English

174

and a marvellous sense of Ulster dialect. I can't believe she'll last; some day somebody will lend her a volume of Grahame Greene and she'll collapse like a balloon ... I really think you should cast an eye over her. She may be only a flash in the pan or she may have something unique and beautiful. If you decide that she's worth anything I'll join in a subscription to buy her a second-hand type-writer; we'll buy her a new one when we're sure she has it in her to go on. She's apparently been entering for competitions, and getting turned down, so you may know of her already. But I wish to God there was anybody with half her talent in Dublin or Cork ...

When I replied to this letter I told O'Connor that Isobel McColl was not unknown to me, that I had already had a few of her stories broadcast, and that in view of his enthusiasm for her work I would have a chat with her. Isobel was a middle-aged, unmarried woman in some kind of domestic service, pleasant looking, dressed plainly and with no thought of fashion, her manner quiet and unassuming, and she had a girlish eagerness to learn. I had invited her to bring along a new story and while we sat having a cup of tea I read it. I thought it disappointing, and when I'd finished it and drunk my tea we fell silent for a while.

'Well, Mr Boyd, what did you think of my story? Do you like it? I hope you do, but of course you may not.'

'Do you like it yourself, Miss McColl?'

'Oh yes, I do. Very much. It's one of my best I think. Don't you?'

Her manner was so shy, her voice so tentative, and her self-assurance so appealing that I did not know how to phrase my reply without depressing her. Finally I spluttered out something about wanting to read it again before coming to a judgement. 'I'm not quite sure that you're studying the right models,' I said, changing the subject slightly. 'What short-story writer do you admire?'

'Oh, I admire Mr O'Connor. I admire him very much. He's a great writer. Have you read his works?'

I said I had.

'And do you agree with me, Mr Boyd?'

I said I did.

'I once wrote to him and showed him some of my own work, and I got a very kind letter back from him. I think he liked my works.'

'I'm glad,' I said. I was also glad that I had not mentioned that O'Connor had written to me too. 'What other writer do you admire, Miss McColl?'

'I read only the best authors, Mr Boyd.'

'Yes, but who are they?' I said, insisting on knowing exactly how far her taste was formed, for she had already confessed to not having much leisure for reading or writing.

Miss McColl did not reply at once. 'Well, Mr Boyd, my favourite writer is Tolstoy. He wrote two works I like very much. Maybe you don't like them. They are called *War and Peace* and *Anna Karenina*. They are both very good.'

I agreed and dropped my enquiries into what models she might use or imitate to advance her career.

I failed both Miss Isobel McColl and O'Connor: she never got even her second-hand typewriter. What happened to her I failed to find out, for I never received another manuscript from her. I do not know whether she ever published any more stories; perhaps she did in some magazine or other, or perhaps she was only 'a flash in the pan' as O'Connor suggested. Anyhow, the incident redounds to O'Connor's credit if not to mine. And I may add that O'Connor himself was a great admirer of Tolstoy and had read *War and Peace* four times. So Miss Isobel McColl and he shared at least one literary model.

All his life, I think, O'Connor felt himself something of an outcast, an outsider, always on the fringe of society. I remember he said to me once, 'You and I will never get invitations to the big houses of this country.' What the context of the remark was I have forgotten – perhaps he was talking of Yeats at Coole – but by a curious coincidence I had recently spent a couple of months with Philip Bell, a well-known architect, visiting half a dozen of the great houses of Ulster, having lunch with their owners, and learning about their histories. O'Connor would have loved this experience, I imagine, chiefly because of his love of architecture. But I refrained from telling him that I had been to these great houses, admittedly as a self-invited guest. After all, it would have been greater fun – at least for me – to have had O'Connor the amateur rather than Bell the professional with me.

I remember one lord of an ancient family who kept questioning me about the BBC: 'Would you mind telling me, Mr Boyd, whether the rumour contains any truth that your organisation is full of communists?' I assured his lordship that the rumour was ill-founded, that the contrary was the case: an answer that appeared to give him some comfort. One of the big houses where I felt at ease was Antrim Castle, probably because the owners appeared to enjoy the chat of Bell and myself. Lord Antrim had once been a speaker in the 'Your Questions' programme and had described himself as feeling like 'a dodo' on that occasion; Lady Antrim, a painter, had appeared in an arts programme. Nevertheless, throughout this architectural tour I was too self-conscious – or class-conscious – to be completely relaxed, and I expect that O'Connor, despite his carapace of confidence, might have had similar feelings if he had been in my place.

I thought of the job of producer – the name itself is significant – as being similar to that of midwife. You persuaded, encouraged, pacified, pleaded, cajoled both ordinary and

177

extraordinary people to give birth to their thoughts by speaking them into a microphone. A storyteller would retell his stories, a poet would repeat his poems, an historian or scientist would popularise his research. Sometimes your hermaphroditic nature permitted you to plant a seed and share in a triumphal birth months later. You were philoprogenitive: but others gave birth. You yourself were paid to remain barren. You became dissatisfied, neurotic, unfulfilled. You worked with artists of all kinds – writers, painters, architects and so on – fell in love with their work, enjoyed yourself, deserted them for a while, shamelessly returned to ask their favours, and fell in love again. You became a glutton for promiscuity and it proved to be an exhausting life.

O'Connor became a teacher of writing in American universities and gloried in his work. I think he must have been a born teacher, but luckily he came to it in middle age and with all the authority of a great writer who had struggled with the problems his pupils would have to face themselves. His trouble, he confessed to me, was that he became too involved in his pupils' own creative efforts. They would try to write stories in his fashion, and in turn he would be irresistibly attracted to the themes they brought to his notice but were themselves quite unable to handle. When he gave me a copy of *The Lonely Voice*, his book on the short story, he inscribed it to 'Another spoiled schoolmaster'. By his own impossibly high standards I suppose he did regard himself as not entirely successful. To be so, he would have wanted to produce a classroom of geniuses! But that he loved the academic atmosphere I have little doubt, for he returned to it again and again. He once remarked to me: 'Kids like you and me, brought up in working-class homes, scrambled into an education. And we want to make up for that, don't we, the rest of our lives with books, painting, music, everything.' He was right: we shared a passion for learning, and a distrust for much of the orthodox education that resulted in degrees and jobs but little else.

My conception of the job I had in the BBC differed, I think, from that held by my superiors, or at least by some of them. I recall that when I joined the Corporation I found that the Head of Programmes had commissioned a long series of twenty-minute talks on Ulster's contribution to the Second World War. The researcher and speaker was George C. Nash, who was a well-known humorist, and secretary of a golf club, but had no real qualifications for such an undertaking. I produced these programmes without any pleasure, the reaction of listeners was minimal, and the only memento I have of the project is a small watercolour of Murlough Bay that George sold to me for £20.

Lynn Doyle and Mat Mulcaghey, two more humorists, were regarded as Ulster's most acceptable radio contribution to litera-ture, aided by a lady of the middle class who called herself 'Mrs Rooney' and provided sketches of her 'amusing' social inferiors. Clearly the local region of the BBC had fixed ideas on how to entertain and inform its listeners. But as these standards were far from my conception of my job I set out to change them. Some-times I thought that perhaps Forrest Reid was right and I should never have left schoolteaching. Still, I was all for taking risks, and Broadcasting House, with its fortress-like façade, was a comfort-able Tower of Babel to inhabit. News from the newsroom, talks from the talks department, features from features, music from the big studio, children in Children's Hour, engineers every-where talking their lingo, and executives in their suites blandly executing: sounds and voices from microphone to transmitter, from studio to sitting room, a modern miracle daily reproduced. The local Great Tower was tilted towards Britain who ruled the airwaves, and we inhabitants were a bit lopsided and lost-looking, living our air-conditioned lives. I belonged to the

Leaning Tower, an outsider inside, who lacked the right accent and didn't always wear the right clothes, and occasionally said the wrong thing at the wrong time. Not that these deviations from the conventional norms disturbed me greatly, though I resented what was virtually a bar to my appearing in front of the microphone: a bar that I disregarded after I had been in the Corporation for about a decade. When I knocked away this obstacle, the opposition made no further protest.

Not until the mid-fifties did I feel myself in full control of the talks department. By this time I had accomplished most of the projects that I had had in mind. I had brought the universities into broadcasting, encouraged as I was by Tom Finnegan of Magee College in Derry and by Eric Ashby who was vice-chancellor of Queen's from 1950 to 1959. Ashby was an excellent speaker who took this minor art seriously and his scripts had the flavour and rhythms of spoken English; he gave a lead to the university which many of his staff followed, so that I was able to invite professors and lecturers from every faculty to talk about their disciplines. The long list of Queen's speakers defeats my memory. Estyn Evans's pupil John Mogey, who left Queen's for Oxford and then the USA, was one. I had old friends from my schooldays such as Jim Beckett the Irish historian, and new friends like the philosopher Bryce Gallie, John Harvey, Larry Lerner, Philip Hobsbaum and Louis Muinzer, all from the English department; later there were Edna and Michael Longley and Seamus Heaney.

Ashby himself believed that popularisation of knowledge was always worthwhile so long as academic standards were maintained. His own *Scientist in Russia*, published by Penguin in 1947, was an excellent example. It was a book I very much admired, for Ashby, besides being a distinguished botanist, was also interested in literature, particularly the great novelists of nineteenth-century Russia: Tolstoy, Turgenev, Chekhov, Dostoevsky, Gogol. As a broadcaster, he was a joy to work with, his approach and style very like Tyrone Guthrie's. And I found his fair-mindedness towards the Soviet Union refreshing: he was a meticulous reporter with a mind disciplined to observe and evaluate facts.

I never sought promotion, nor was I offered it. Indeed I thought that being a producer was the most interesting work the BBC could offer, and it was well paid – at least by my standards. Once I applied for a six months' broadcasting post in Sri Lanka but I failed to get it; this failure did not upset me as I was able to spend a couple of days in London with Bill Naughton and a day in the company of Deirdre, our daughter, who was then living in Essex and attending a training college for primary school teachers.

In 1959, soon after this failure to see the Orient – one of my never-realised ambitions – I was compensated by getting on a six months' television training course in London. This I had to fight for and had to appeal to the then Controller, the amiable Bob McCall, that I was being discriminated against for efficiency. My appeal proved successful.

On the whole, I spent a refreshing six months. The lectures and demonstrations were full of interest, I conscientiously attended them, and most evenings I was free to explore London.

I remember that when Louis MacNeice heard I was in London on the course he tried half a dozen times to contact me for a drink or a meal. But as I was preoccupied with television lectures and projects I felt disinclined to spend any of my free evenings in the company of colleagues in the BBC – even Louis, whose company I enjoyed. MacNeice was a prodigious worker who, like many such, always gave the impression to his friends that he had plenty of leisure for them, and when we finally did meet – quite

181

by accident – in a pub, he snarled a greeting: 'What d'you mean by not getting in touch with me? What's the matter with you?'

I had no real answer for him and muttered something about being out of sorts.

'Bertie tried to get in touch with you as well,' he added. Then, having told me off he appeared to forgive me, warning me that Rodgers was after my blood. I was flattered that both had tried to seek me out, imagining that I might be lonely; but I seldom was with so many London theatres, cinemas and concerts to choose from. When I felt like company I usually phoned Bill Naughton, a more lively conversationalist than either Louis or Bertie, with a greater sense of fun and more Irish in his humour. Indeed, when Bill, Frank O'Connor and I were together the three of us would be completely relaxed, whereas with Louis, Bertie and myself the flow of chat sometimes came to a halt and alcohol was required to start it flowing again.

My digs were in the home of an elderly Jewish woman from Vienna, Mrs Grauberg, who looked after me well but did not like me to stay out too late at night, being fearful of what might happen to me – and to herself, because when her front door remained unprotected by its locks and chains she was unable to go asleep. The days of the Nazi terror against the Jews still haunted her and she felt vulnerable when alone in her well-furnished house in Hamlet Gardens in Hammersmith. Mrs Grauberg was a generous and thoughtful widow who thought I must be lonely and therefore suggested that I invite Elizabeth and our two sons, Brian and Gavin, to stay for a week or so. For a short period my digs became home and I realised how much a married and family man I was, though I am not fond of the phrase 'a well-knit family'. Indeed I dislike it: much better for a family to be loosely knit with each member having fresh air to breathe and space to grow up as individuals. Perhaps I saw too little of our three children as they were growing up; if so, I think it better to err on that side rather than to risk suffocating them with the paternal presence. As our three children grew up they became more and more independent of both Elizabeth and myself, made their own marriages and careers, and all are now living in England.

By the time I did my television course my younger brother Jimmy had left the *Irish Times* in Dublin for a job in the news department of the BBC in London. This gave me great pleasure because though we met irregularly, we enjoyed each other's company, and for both of us to be in broadcasting gave us another common interest. Like myself, Jimmy was a home bird; though he liked London he preferred Belfast, and after some rejections he got his way and returned home. He, Vera his wife, and Kevin his son, helped to cement my attachment to Belfast: our loosely knit family had been added to, and I gained a tennis opponent whose skill was no better than my own. Jimmy's world was not mine, however: he liked the company of journalists such as Bud Bossence of the *Belfast News-Letter* and the habitués of the Duke of York bar where they congregated. I had no interest in newspaper gossip so I rarely went there, and always with Jimmy. In the BBC building itself we seldom met, except by chance in the corridor where we would greet each other with a nod or a 'hello'. This casualness seemed natural to us and many of the staff were unaware that we were brothers. But our affection for each other was deep – not only affection but respect – and when he died suddenly from an embolism at the age of fifty-three I felt numbed. A part of myself had gone.

Jimmy died in 1976. He was in the middle of his BBC career and held the post of Assistant Head of News.

9

Nearly every day immediately after lunch I used to wander about the Belfast streets – the docks, the bookshops in Smithfield, the back streets of the Lower Falls and Shankill, the Belfast and County Down railway station into which my father shunted his trains many thousands of times from early morning to late at night, returning home pale from weariness, his face streaked with oil. Sometimes I went into a pub, deserted in the early afternoon, to leaf over a second-hand book I had bought or just to sit for half an hour in silence. Occasionally I would go into St George's Church at the Albert Clock or the Catholic church in Chapel Lane, find a pew and rest. I had no religious faith, no belief in prayer, felt no need to worship a God or accept a creed. I suppose this should have cut me off, in some vital way, from many of my friends and acquaintances, but I do not think it did. I very seldom discussed religion with anyone except those whose attitude more or less coincided with my own – and that made for dullness – while to discuss it with fervent believers I always found a waste of time, like two people trying to conduct a debate but unable to understand each other's language. Long ago I reached the conclusion that a great many people who

184

believe themselves to be, for example, Christians, give only lip service to their belief and lead lives of self-delusion. Neither the people of the Catholic South nor those of mainly Protestant Northern Ireland seem to me much different from the people of agnostic England in the spiritual quality of their daily existence, at least to judge from the quality of their press, television or radio, to which they devote more concentration than they do to their faiths.

The BBC in Northern Ireland tried hard to find an identity which would be acceptable to Protestant unionists and nationalist Catholics but I think it failed: programmes were too often a mishmash which satisfied neither. Of course many good programmes were made by people like Sam Hanna Bell, who had a deep and wide knowledge of the Northern way of life, by Edgar Boucher and Havelock Nelson (both from the South) who had a love of Irish music, and perhaps by some others. The great demerit of the place during most of my time there was the exclusion of Catholics from the senior staff: not a single producer belonged to that faith. Once, in a casual conversation with Richard Marriott, the Controller from 1953 to 1956, I mentioned this as a fact. He was incredulous. 'I don't believe you,' he said. 'It can't be true.' I repeated that it *was* true. He left me, a worried look on his face. Soon afterwards a Catholic was appointed to the news department, and from that time onwards I think religious discrimination began to disappear.

I enjoyed Marriott's confidence and never doubted his integrity: any kind of injustice was abhorrent to him, and I was certain he would root it out once he had convinced himself of its presence. Unfortunately Marriott returned too soon to London and the more liberal attitudes that prevailed there. He was, I am certain, the best man who ever held the post of Controller in Northern Ireland, and I was proud to retain his friendship until his death not long after his retirement. An Oxford graduate, fond of history and French, he would have fitted well into a senior common room. I do not mean to suggest, however, that he did not fit well into the upper echelons of the BBC. He did. And unquestionably he gained everyone's respect for his conscientiousness, his sense of justice and his quiet sense of humour. He was not a good mixer – controllers, like headmasters, were expected to be aloof from their staff – but on occasions he could be persuaded to unbend. I once invited him to the Elbow Room for a drink, arguing that it was his duty to familiarise himself with the social habits of his subordinates. I remember the occasion because when he appeared in the saloon bar upstairs alone and looked round I waved for him to join the table where I was sitting with a couple of producers and James Boyce, who was then a very popular broadcaster. We were discussing what was 'U' and 'non-U' speech according to Nancy Mitford in an article she contributed to the *New Statesman*, I think; this article contained lists of alternative words, one being characteristic of upper-class usage, the other of the lower orders. We had been testing one another's U-ability: 'glasses' or 'spectacles', 'toilet' or 'lavatory', and so on. I had done badly, choosing the non-U word in preference to the U word ten times out of twenty. Marriott agreed to join in the silly game.

'I'm bound to get the U word every time,' he said seriously and self-mockingly. He was twenty times right.

'I told you so, didn't I?' Then he added, 'But I think Miss Mitford is wrong in one instance, as I suspected she would be.' I have forgotten what the instance was – it did not matter to me, but clearly it did to him. Yet I do not believe Marriott was a snob: he was an upper-middle-class Englishman who knew his place in the social ladder and could do nothing about it even if he had wanted to – which he did not. I think he never again patronised the Elbow Room, but that visit had a sequel. One day he summoned me to his large office on the first floor.

'I hope I'm not interrupting your work,' he began.

I assured him I was not busy.

'You are my *éminence grise*,' he said. I felt flattered. 'Well, you know the place much better than I do – or ever will. So I want to ask your opinion about something.' He paused.

'Important?' I queried.

'Could be ... could be ... I don't know,' he went on, puffing away at his cigarette. 'I think this region of the BBC should have a club – a sort of social club. We could acquire premises very near – just round the corner in fact. Would you approve of the idea?'

I gave an unsatisfactory answer: I neither approved nor disapproved; I thought privately that I already spent too much time in the BBC and confessed to being not much of a clubman myself.

'You think I'm foolish,' he said. 'Is that it? The club would have a licence, of course.' Clearly he had made up his mind to have his social club and as I left him he smiled and thanked me. 'Perhaps it'll be known as Marriott's Folly.'

It proved to be successful, but few who use it now have ever heard of Richard Marriott, its 'onlie begetter'. My suspicion is that at the back of his mind, or perhaps unconsciously, he had a notion of civilising the under-civilised in this untamed Irish province that was foreign territory to him. Incidentally he also unearthed from the BBC vaults a sum of money to buy the paintings of local artists to adorn the bleak corridors of the building. Most important of all, he initiated a thinktank of a group of producers which met monthly on Saturday mornings to exchange ideas about future programmes. Marriott attended it, the Head of Programmes reluctantly chaired it, and it was abandoned immediately Marriott was transferred to London.

Obviously new ideas – which could be dangerous – were no longer to be welcomed.

I think Marriott was disappointed when I refused his offer to follow him to London, but whenever I visited London I usually called at his office in Broadcasting House for a chat. Although he was Director of Home Broadcasting, his office was much smaller than the one he had as Controller in Belfast, and he seemed to me to have diminished in importance. This was of course an illusion – the big fish in a small pond illusion. Clearly my preference was for the small pond. As always, I found him the conscientious official, refusing to leave his office until he had dutifully listened to the six o'clock news. Once reassured that all was well with the world he would say cheerfully, 'Well, let's go now. Where'll we go for a drink? Or would you like to come home with me for a meal?' I never accepted this invitation, almost sure that it arose from politeness, for I knew that, like myself, he kept his home private and did not encourage casual callers. Only after his retirement did I visit his house in Hampstead and then I was aware of his illness. We talked of Proust but he admitted he was beyond reading anything in French, or even in English, his memory was so impaired. When he died several years ago, I too was in retirement from the BBC and, as the phrase goes, 'out of touch', so I never learned of his death until nearly a year later.

I think Dick Marriott – it took me years to call him by his familiar Christian name – envied me the life I led as a producer and later as a playwright. He himself greatly admired 'creative people' as he called them, and liked me to talk about the writers and artists I was friendly with. I arranged for him to buy a couple of paintings by Markey Robinson; at that time only about twenty people patronised Markey's work. Our patronage was far from generous, however, for Markey sold his pictures for five or ten pounds each, sometimes perhaps a few pounds more. He must have painted hundreds to keep himself alive, and for many years he lived in poverty. Markey had the reputation of being capable of biting the hands that fed him, and if he did so it was understandable: the hands – mine among them – exploited him. For years now he has lived in Dublin and is seen sometimes in the streets wheeling a pram loaded with his work. How good a painter Markey is I cannot judge: all I know is that a couple of the paintings I own have given me lasting pleasure. One is of a Parisian *place* (Markey used to make occasional trips to France, disappearing for months at a time and returning with fantastic tales of the women he had met); this is a highly complex, Utrillo-like painting which I treasure; the other one is of a group of quarry workers on a dark mountainside, their figures as stiff and monumental as the granite they are quarrying.

Markey used to roam the streets of Belfast endlessly, walking quickly with his loping stride as if hurrying to some urgent appointment, but I would be surprised if he had many urgent appointments to keep, for if he met me or any of his acquaintances he would halt at once and start on a harangue about somebody who was persecuting him – usually some Ministry of Labour official who wanted to withdraw his weekly dole on the grounds that he was employed.

'They won't let me paint! They don't want me to paint! They don't want Art! But their day won't last much longer. ... It can't! What kind of people are they? Tell me that! Can you now? What *are* they? You should know ... You meet them. You say you don't know? But you do ... only you won't tell me ... But I'll tell you what they are ... all of them ... The Government, the Corporation, the Arts Council, the BBC ... all of them ... the lot ... And you're one of them yourself ... you all sit in yer fat arses an' do nothin' fur nobody ... Now don't luk at me like that ... I know you've been a good friend of mine. I know that ... But why

189

are you all doin' the same to me? Tell me why! Why? Tell me why! You must know.' If he was carrying a picture, wrapped in newspaper or in brown paper, under his arm he would ask me to have a look at it and we would go into a café for a cup of tea. Once or twice I remember he was made unwelcome until I explained he was my guest. But he did not allow these minor rebuffs to upset him in the least – I suppose he was used to them. After I had examined his picture he would say, 'Well, what d'you think of it? Isn't it good? It's one of my best, you know, an' I'm only askin' ... Tell me, what d'you think it's worth?'

Sometimes I bought his pictures, sometimes I didn't, explaining that I had no more room on the walls – a limp excuse, of course, but I found it hard to think of another.

'What about your friends? You've plenty of them, haven't you?'

I admitted I had, and Markey already knew that some of them, like Frank O'Connor, Bill Naughton, Dick Marriott, Frances Jackson, Diana Hyde, Sam Bell and others, had bought his work. I liked and admired Markey, and he knew I did; but sometimes when I caught sight of him in the street I crossed to the other side, and sometimes when he called at the BBC I was unavailable. A painter in Belfast can very rarely scrape a livelihood, and eventually Markey had to leave for Dublin.

Willie Conor was one of the few that survived, living frugally and picking up occasional commissions. Markey too lived frugally but I think he found few commissions. Once he brought me to his kitchen house to view some paintings and to examine his collection of toy soldiers, which he had spread out on his table. He insisted that I should drink a glass of wine which obviously had been bought for the occasion – he himself did not drink and I swallowed his wine with difficulty – then I realised that what we were doing was having a little private view – *un vernissage* –

in the back street of Belfast where he was living alone, his wife and daughter having left him for Canada. Markey's little *vernissage* was not very different from the evening Willie Conor and I spent in his little studio on the Stranmillis Road opposite the Museum and Art Gallery. I did not know Willie as well as I knew Markey but I took an instant liking to him the first time I met him (during the Second World War) in Campbell's café where at a table upstairs people like Denis Ireland, Joe Tomelty, Sam Bell, Richard Rowley and others met on Saturday mornings for literary, theatrical and artistic gossip.

Conor always refused invitations to talk about his work in a BBC studio but when I suggested to him that I could bring a portable recording machine to his Stranmillis studio and that we might have a chat and let the reel run on he agreed, much to my surprise. When I arrived, Willie explained that everything was in a mess, for he was clearing up because he had to leave his studio. The reason for his departure I never learned – whether for his own convenience or the convenience of the landlord. Willie was not communicative, at least to me, in personal matters. But he appeared to be in his usual good spirits.

Suspecting he might be nervous before the recording began I had armed myself with a bottle of whiskey. A completely sober recording session can be a stilted one, especially if the victim has never before faced the ordeal. We had a couple of drinks to loosen Willie's tongue, then we recorded, Willie replying to my questions about himself and his work in his slightly hesitant and completely unpretentious style. It was a short interview and afterwards we relaxed.

'Do painters enjoy this carry-on?' he asked me with his giggle.

'Some do and some don't,' I said. 'Most of them don't, I think.'

'I'm not surprised.'

'Stanley Spencer is an exception. He went on talking for about forty minutes without stopping, though I wanted only a ten-minute interview. I hadn't to ask him a question at all – he just started on his childhood in Cookham and hardly drew a breath.'

'Was it good?'

'Very. He enjoyed himself. Then he asked for a playback, saying he'd never heard his own voice.'

'I've never heard mine and I don't want to either. Has Stanley a good voice?'

'Not very. High-pitched and squeaky, but very fluent. Words come easily to him.'

'So I've been told. Did he like the sound of his voice when he first heard it?'

'Yes. He thought he'd a beautiful voice. But of course he hadn't. People usually hate their voices the first time, then they become used to them and often get to like them. Stanley just loved his voice.'

'Stanley's a curious wee man. A good painter. Very good, no doubt about it. You've seen that one – *Resurrection* – in the gallery across the road? I like it … I like it very much.'

We went on talking about Spencer and I told Willie how melancholy Stanley became when we went to the Elbow Room afterwards. He drank lemonade and said he was unhappy because of his sex life. Then he quickly departed. He wanted to speak to his niece Daphne, a beautiful girl who then worked as a secretary in the BBC. He was fond of Daphne – as I was too – and I was glad when she married my colleague Johnny Robinson, an excellent journalist. I was sorry when they both left Belfast many years later to live in Dorset.

That autumn day in Willie's studio was the first – and the last – time we were alone; we met a few times afterwards but in company. Our meeting at 13A Stranmillis Road was to me memorable though Willie didn't talk much and I talked too much. When the light from the glass roof began to fade and Willie had finally tidied up, we left. Before leaving I picked up from the floor a watercolour of Lisburn Cathedral which Willie was throwing out.

'I mind the day I painted that,' he said. 'It was on the 19th July 1912. I mind it was a good day.'

'For me too,' I said. 'It was the day I was born.'

I wanted to buy the watercolour but Willie insisted on giving it to me, explaining that he was only going to tear it up – and he had actually begun to do so, for there is a little tear at the bottom. Whether he lacked the heart to finish the job or whether I interrupted him when I arrived at his studio I do not know.

For some reason or other I have never had a close friendship with any painter, either man or woman. I have been on terms of acquaintanceship with half a dozen or more painters – Colin Middleton, George Campbell, Gerry Dillon, George MacCann and his wife Mercy, Tom Carr, Terry Flanaghan, Dan O'Neill and so on; and I have admired their work, but I have never shared the relationship with any one of them that comes naturally when I meet a writer whose work appeals to me. This is very strange, for writers are very critical indeed of one another and seldom dole out undiluted praise. Indeed they often take a perverse pleasure in discovering weaknesses in the work of their peers. Though I have been able to encourage some struggling writers by accepting their work for broadcasting, I have also been over-critical of their efforts and impatient when their progress has proved to be sluggish or disappointing.

One exception springs to my mind. John O'Connor was the most promising young writer I ever met. I first met him in the Elbow Room with Sam Bell who had invited him to Belfast to discuss an idea for a feature programme. Like me, Sam was always on the lookout for new writers, especially if they were young and working-class. John O'Connor was under thirty, lived in Armagh, was unemployed, and had high ambitions. He was therefore the ideal protégé for Sam and me, and we both thought that if things went all right John would be able to fulfil himself. Things did not turn out all right: John was unable to find a steady job in Ireland, emigrated to Australia, and died before he was forty. He had published some short stories and a novel, *Come Day – Go Day*. That was all: and it was not enough. Far from it. *Come Day – Go Day* – a beautifully written account of working-class poverty in Armagh – was a remarkable achievement and sufficient proof that John O'Connor, if he had lived, would have become a notable Irish novelist.

He had little formal education and when I once asked him who or what started him off writing he replied in one word, 'O'Flaherty'. He had picked up a volume of Liam O'Flaherty's stories in the local library, read them enthusiastically and said to himself, 'I could do as well as that.' And sometimes perhaps he did. Certainly, like O'Flaherty, he was a natural writer and when he was at his best and writing without strain he wrote with complete authenticity. Occasionally, again like O'Flaherty, he became self-conscious and overwrote.

I was wholly sympathetic with John O'Connor's aspirations and eager that he should succeed, but I – and Sam Bell too – could give him only limited help. What we could not give him was what he needed most: a regular job. Without that his future was precarious. He became a temporary postman – his elder brother was in the Post Office – he started a small local paper which collapsed after a few issues, and he once left Armagh on a bicycle for a tour of Spain, France and Italy, writing articles about his adventures. A bicycle company presented him with his bicycle as an advertisement for their machine, I commissioned a radio talk, and during his tour he took all sorts of jobs on farms and in hotels to help him on his way. Sometimes he gave blood in exchange for a night's bed and breakfast in a hospital. He was fit when he cycled from Armagh and even fitter when he returned home, bronzed and full of stories. But once he had experienced life on the shores of the Mediterranean he was unable to settle down again to the life offered him at home, so he left like thousands of Irishmen before him, and Ireland lost a writer. When in 1984 the Blackstaff Press published a new edition of *Come Day – Go Day*, Sam Bell contributed a short memoir of John O'Connor, and Ben Kiely praised the novel in the *Irish Times*. I accompanied Michael Burns and Anne Tannahill, his publishers, to Armagh to talk about John and his work. The Museum and Art Gallery in the Mall was crammed full; John's old friends reminisced about him, and about a hundred copies of the novel were sold. Of course, it was a posthumous triumph: a young man of literary talent who should have been cherished in his lifetime by his native city had at last, years after his death far from home, received the recognition he deserved. Rough justice had been done, but too late. It was not enough. It seldom is in Ireland.

But at least John O'Connor is not forgotten.

10

I am what is called a 'rooted' writer, that is, I have stuck gluelike
to my native city. Even worse – or better – I have stuck to that part
of it I know best and where I was born and brought up: Ballymacarrett and its environs. Ballymacarrett is mostly a working-class
area overlooked by the shipyards, and the place where I was
born – in Baskin Street, off Templemore Avenue – is right at its
heart. My topographical moves, however, have always been
upwards and outwards. My father never had any social ambitions except to rent a house with a good bathroom so that he
could clean himself up after coming home from work on the
railway in his dirty dungarees. And my mother at least shared
that modest ambition. A bathroom did not interest me much but
a room of my own did. By the time I got to the university we had
all satisfied our ambitions and moved a mile or so from the heart
of Ballymacarrett. About twenty years ago, after various zigzag
moves, long married now and my father and mother both dead,
I settled for good in Ballynafeigh – about three miles from where
I was born – but in the suburbs and in an avenue from where I
could see the contours of the Antrim as well as the Cregagh and
Castlereagh hills. I ask for no better view.

I am attached to Belfast by my lifelong familiarity with its sights and sounds – by the narrow back streets and ubiquitous corner shops in the east, by a few suburban avenues in the south, by the River Lagan at the Queen's Bridge, the Albert Bridge, the Ormeau Bridge, the King's Bridge, the Governor's Bridge, each encompassing a different segment or circle of the city, like rings of a cut-down tree, the inner rings beginning to rot. All the bridges – with the exception of Ormeau – are unimaginatively named, like the plethora of Belfast streets called after Queen Victoria. Belfast is a Victorian, mainly Protestant city which protests its Protestantism loudly and too often for its own moral good. I am also detached and distanced from my native place and its dominant tradition, and estranged from its materialistic values and its raucous bigotry. All the same I have found it no hardship to stay, unlike some of my friends, particularly writers. John Hewitt, though, was one who, on his retirement, chose to return home and soon found himself recognised as the father-figure of the younger poets such as Seamus Heaney, James Simmons, Derek Mahon – all the nestlings nurtured by a young, energetic academic from Queen's called Philip Hobsbaum who not only wrote poetry himself but tried to turn everybody he met into a poet. If Philip did not always succeed he at least implanted in the heads of many young people an understanding that poetry lived outside text books and was an enduring activity not to be neglected if their lives were to be worth living. But Philip left Belfast for academic preferment in Glasgow and left his nestlings to grow up, and a few flew away to America or London or Dublin.

John Hewitt, the most 'Ulster' of writers, was a likable man once you got to know him, but he took some knowing. I certainly did not get to know him well until the last decade of his life – he died in 1987 just before he reached the age of eighty, a whitebearded, patriarchal figure – and the more I knew him the more I liked him, and his poetry too. His faults of character were the minor ones that nearly all of us share, especially writers: vanity and self-centredness; but his patent honesty and integrity shone forth during all the time I was acquainted with him, first of all as a young, portly, self-important museum official with a chubby face, and finally as an old man full of dignity and honour, benign if occasionally sharp-tongued, who walked slowly and with difficulty, his feet splayed widely apart the better to keep his precarious balance. I thought he lectured well and read poetry badly, but after somebody told me that my own reading of poetry was not unlike Hewitt's I changed my opinion. I also changed my opinion of his verse (as he modestly referred to it). I found much of the early work prosaic and stilted as well as technically unadventurous, and I thought it strange that a radical thinker, full of Marx and Engels, Morris and Shaw, should be content within the confines of conventional forms and language. But as the years passed and as I met John more frequently I came to the conclusion that he was an extremely conventional person who lived conventionally, dressed conventionally and behaved conventionally; indeed his carefully turned verse faithfully reflected the carefully turned-out public figure. In this regard he was the antithesis of T.S. Eliot, a conservatively minded man who loosened up the conventional poetry of his time. I take it as axiomatic that suffering is necessary for the production of good poetry: human suffering of flesh and spirit, the kind of suffering that Gerard Manley Hopkins released in his sonnet with its anguish:

> Thou art indeed just, Lord, if I contend
> With thee; but, sir, so what I plead is just.

Hewitt once confessed that he was near to suicide after having been turned down for the job of Director of the Belfast Museum and Art Gallery; it was of course a severe blow to his pride but hardly, I thought, an excuse for such an act, involving, as it would have involved, extreme distress to his wife Roberta who loved him dearly and protected him like a mother her child. It was Roberta's death in 1975 that caused John to write his most deeply felt poems; more than any other event in his life Roberta's death caused him to suffer deeply; otherwise perhaps his life was too comfortable.

For many years as a young and middle-aged man, Hewitt stood his ground in the North of Ireland dedicating himself to the art and craft of poetry, to criticism of painting, and to the study of politics. At one time he was a fervent Marxist, but if his fervour withered he never denied – at least to my knowledge – the importance and relevance of Marxism; about a year before his death I can recall a discussion with him about Gramsci and the possibility of socialism in Italy. Yet much of the fire had burned itself out, quenched by the revelations of the evils of Stalinism. He no longer saw the Soviet Union as a beacon of light and he had been unable to replace that vision. We never, I think, discussed the 'Troubles' at home, probably because we had nothing illuminating to say to each other about them. The time had come for endurance, for staying put, for waiting and watching. He threw his waning energy into his poetry, his trusteeship of the Lyric Theatre and his enjoyment of friendship. He could well say with Hazlitt that his life had been a happy one, and one of affirmation.

Changing the tense of the verb, I could say the same for myself. I was as happy as anyone could be in a part of Ireland cut off from the main part of the island and trying obstinately to persuade itself that it was British. The Catholics in the North, of course, needed no persuasion as to their identity: they were Irish and proud of it and proclaimed their Irishness at every opportunity. I felt more at ease with them than with most of my Protestant friends, and increasingly so in my middle age. Unlike John Hewitt I entertained no doubts about my identity: I was Irish and that simply was that. The fact that I was not a Catholic did not concern me in the least; no more than it would have concerned a Protestant Frenchman like André Gide or a French Jew like Léon Blum to doubt his nationality. I thought that John made an unnecessary fuss about something he should have decided for himself before he left school. For in my own schooldays I *felt* Irish despite all the British propaganda in song and story drummed into me. Not that I did not enjoy it: of course I did. I loved to stand and sing 'God Save the King', for instance, because I loved to sing anything at all and had no taste whatsoever for music or anything else. Then too I was a Wolf Cub and a Boy Scout and accepted the imperialist saga in the same way as I would accept a fairytale. It was as if I was made of putty and could be moulded into any shape.

But time passed, I read many books of my own choosing and I became what I was – a Belfast youngster born and bred into a working-class family, discontented with the poverty and roughness of my environment and determined to get an education that would hoist me out of it. England, Scotland and Wales were 'across the water' and different countries entirely; but the South of Ireland was separated from the North merely by a mysterious wriggling border that caused a lot of trouble and argument though hardly anybody seemed to know where exactly it was. It divided fields and streams and villages and appeared to do no good to anybody except smugglers.

I grew up learning very little Irish history and what little I did learn seemed to me not of much interest. English history was much more interesting because it had good and bad kings and queens, princes and princesses, aristocrats and nobles, lords and ladies, and best of all an empire that spread all over the world and was coloured red on the map. I thought it a pity that Ireland had nothing romantic like all that to offer, nothing except battles at Clontarf and the Yellow Ford and sieges at Derry and Limerick and, most important of all, the famous battle of the Boyne in 1690. We Protestants were supposed to be on the side of William of Orange, but although I thought orange lilies were beautiful and I was fond of the colour orange probably because I loved oranges, I failed to summon up enthusiasm for a stern-looking Dutchman on a white horse crossing an Irish river. I preferred the horse to the rider with his unsmiling unfriendly face, and only wished I could get hold of such a steed myself. What this Dutchman was doing in Ireland I could never understand; nor King James either, a dim figure who seemed to me no better than King William.

So obviously the thousands of Orangemen who walked through the streets of Belfast carrying banners of King William had much more interest in Irish history than I had, and took the subject much more seriously too.

As broadcasting was such an ephemeral medium and as I was anxious to salvage from the hundreds of programmes I had initiated something of academic value, I planned to have three books published by the BBC in Northern Ireland. All three would be histories: they were *Ulster Since 1800: a political and economic survey* (1954), *Ulster Since 1800: a social survey* (1957), both edited by T.W. Moody and J.C. Beckett, and *Belfast: the origin and growth of an industrial city* (1967) edited by J.C. Beckett and R.E. Glasscock. The origin of these volumes was unorthodox and slightly conspiratorial. I had some friends among the members of the BBC General Advisory Committee who on their way to their important meetings in the Board Room (with food and drink provided to dissipate their critical sense) had made a habit of calling in at my office and whispering, 'Is there anything you'd like brought up?' I suggested the two Ulster histories to David Kennedy and J.J. Campbell, both of them regarded as 'liberal Catholics' in the BBC, and both influential figures in the community. We agreed that the editors should be two distinguished Protestant historians, Moody of Trinity and Beckett of Queen's. I had been to Inst with both. The suggestion won the approval of the committee, the two volumes proved to be popular and were of course authoritative, with both Campbell and Kennedy among the contributors, though I need hardly say there was no collusion about their inclusion. Everything went smoothly, the various historians wrote their talks, which became chapters of the books and printing began. Then we hit a snag. I was told by Robert Crossett, the Assistant Head of Programmes, that the Religious Advisory Committee had disapproved of the usage 'Catholics' for 'Roman Catholics' and that the editors would have to be informed of this decision. I informed them. Moody at once replied that he and Beckett had decided to follow the practice of the Oxford University Press which was to use the term 'Roman Catholic' initially and ever afterwards the term 'Catholic'. That they had done. So the objection was dropped. Indeed it would have taken a brave clergyman to oppose Theo Moody on such a point, for I never met a more scrupulous scholar or more dignified man, with his tall, erect figure, his severe face which reminded me of some Italian prelate, and his slight stammer as he carefully chose his words. He and Jim Beckett were ideal editors and working with them gave me insight into what real scholarship meant.

The other project I was proud of – though I was not responsible for the idea – was the making of an LP selection of Frank

O'Connor's broadcasts. This was a joint production between Christopher Holme working in London and myself working in Belfast. Holme had produced two programmes from *Kings, Lords and Commons*, O'Connor's translations from the Gaelic, and I had produced two earlier programmes – 'The Idealist', one of O'Connor's best stories of childhood, and 'One Man's Way', his talk about the art of the short story. To realise my own part in this project I had to confess to being guilty of an irregularity. Knowing that I had produced many O'Connor broadcasts from Belfast, Holme arrived to find out how many records or tapes had been stored in our archives. To his surprise he found that all had been destroyed or 'wiped'. I was summoned to the Head of Programmes office.

'I've just been telling Mr Holme that unfortunately we haven't retained any of O'Connor's broadcasts owing to lack of space in our archives,' he explained.

'Oh, but I retained copies for myself,' I confessed at once.

'But that is quite irregular.'

'Yes, I know. I plead guilty.'

'Well, Mr Holme, you're lucky after all!'

I was given a mild reprimand for my misconduct, Holme returned to London and the selection was made. I only wish now that I had been guilty of more 'irregularities' of a similar kind.

I have mentioned what I think back on as successes: occasions when I have bucked the system or situation and got away with it. But I also had failures of one kind or another: occasions when I kept silent on some controversy instead of speaking out, or when I accepted censorship under its polite name of editorialisation (or some equally horrible euphemism), or when I accepted decisions which I should have opposed. For instance, I sought the help of Agnes Finnegan, the wife of Professor Tom Finnegan of Magee College, to get a properly balanced audience in Derry for a 'Your Questions' programme, promising her that the Catholics would be encouraged to speak out and would not be cut out of the recorded edition. Some *were* edited out despite my protest, but I did not protest enough. I should have threatened resignation: or indeed I ought to have resigned. For years Agnes – a forgiving woman – found my surrender to authority hard to forgive, and rightly so. I had failed her; the BBC had failed me. There was another occasion when Menna Gallie, a novelist and broadcaster, had her script on Northern Ireland (actually a contribution to the Welsh service) censored in Belfast and passages deleted as being too controversial, as 'dangerous thoughts'. I was present when the excisions were communicated to the Gallies and felt ashamed to be on the side of the Corporation by keeping silent when I should have expressed my fury. Menna burst into tears; Bryce, her husband, Professor of Philosophy at Queen's, raised his voice in protest and would have lost his temper if he had been less rational by temperament and training.

These are relatively minor examples of censorship, of blunting the sharp edges of controversy and allowing the Unionist Party to sit complacently in power in Stormont. In my view, the BBC failed to reflect the objective social conditions that prevailed in Northern Ireland, and its timidity was inexcusable. I think that everybody responsible for programmes bears guilt: the senior staff from controllers down to producers (not excluding advisory committees and Northern Ireland 'national' governors!). Problems like unemployment, housing and religious discrimination were of course mentioned *en passant* in certain programmes but never given adequate treatment.

I belonged to the establishment without adhering to it. There are many talented civil servants, BBC officials, Arts Council people, academics and so on: intelligent, progressively minded men and women who have the liberty to go a certain distance, but no further. Many others are dull conformists. I remember one BBC Controller proclaiming to his staff with all the dignity he could command, 'The fabric of the State must be preserved.' He was right of course, but wrong to consider that it was his responsibility to preserve it. When I joined the Corporation the pro-unionist bias of the local station was undeniable – though it was of course denied – and we producers were expected not to challenge it. Few of us did. But slowly, too slowly, with the coming of new controllers the bias was straightened: Andrew Stewart helped, then Dick Marriott, and then Waldo Maguire, the first Irishman to hold the post. Energetic, self-confident and completely lacking in pomposity, Waldo (as everybody called him) took off his jacket and worked in his shirtsleeves, a small burly incongruous figure in his big office. He looked out of place there and often rushed to the news offices where he seemed to be much more at home. He worked hard and the job almost killed him; after suffering a stroke when out fishing one weekend his retirement was inevitable. I have no idea what his own politics were but he certainly never allowed himself to be influenced by any local politician.

I have written so much about my BBC work because so much of my time for twenty-five years was devoted to my job. I thought it one of the most interesting and demanding jobs possible; it gave me a great deal of satisfaction (and some annoyances of course) but I also thought that I had sacrificed something I greatly valued – a sense of freedom, of being able to live the kind of life I would ideally desire. I was sacrificing the best years of my life doing what I would certainly not do from choice. Yet the rewards were great, and the chief of these were the opportunities I had to make friends. I made so many – and they were so different in background and temperament – that I reached the conclusion that I had a gift for friendship. If so, it is a gift I'm lucky to possess: but I can take little credit for it and do not think I possessed it when young. My few friendships at school were transitory affairs, unlike the friendships I have made in adult life.

Although I had to spend most of my time in the BBC building either in my own office for clerical work or in the studios for productions, I liked to leave the building for OBs – Outside Broadcasts – accompanied by a couple of engineers. Indeed I preferred the company of engineers to that of programme staff. They were less pretentious and more efficient, and were regarded as second-class servants of the Corporation because of their association with manual duties. Most of them had accents which betrayed their working-class origin, while the tone of the BBC itself was definitely middle-class; the tone was set by the staff in the higher echelons, and imitation of their mores was the sincerest form of flattery.

The engineer I knew best was Bob Haldane, who was probably the most popular person on the staff of the BBC in Northern Ireland. A white-haired, ruddy-faced, smiling man, Bob never seemed out of humour with himself or the world; but although he looked healthy he had to attend hospital regularly for an abdominal weakness which he never referred to because of shyness. Always engaged on OBs, Bob travelled thousands of miles every year in his recording van with its bulky gear, so his friends were scattered all over the North, in farms, villages and towns. Bob often returned to Belfast laden with farm produce he had bought or been given on his 'trips', as he called them. His hobby was composing verse, which he wrote on loose pages and brought into my office for perusal.

'Just tell me how it sounds to you,' he would begin. 'I know

it's not very good, but I like writing it. It does no harm, does it?'
And he would grin. Occasionally one of his lyrics would be
published in a local paper or magazine and he would enter my
office beaming with pleasure, like a child given a new toy.
Indeed, Bob's nature struck me as extraordinarily innocent as if
he had never completely grown up. He never spoke of his
experiences with the Royal Flying Corps in the First World War
and when I asked him what flying was like in the pioneering
days he would reply with an 'Ach, don't ask me: I've almost
forgotten.' And the subject would be changed. Though he was
the best ambassador the BBC ever had in Ireland, his name is
hardly, if at all, remembered: his status was not grand enough.
When he retired he haunted the building for a year or so, then
gradually his visits came to an end; when he died I was away on
holiday and so missed his funeral.

Bob gave me the idea for one of the most successful programmes I ever compiled. His sister Una had married an Italian
lawyer called Mario, lived in Italy during the Mussolini regime
and spent the years of the Second World War there. Both were
anti-fascist and during the war Una, who had been accustomed
to writing home every week, was unable to do so. But her habit
was so strong and gave her so much pleasure that she continued
writing her letters though they could not be posted home;
instead they were hidden in a safe place until the war ended and
then the collection was brought back to Belfast. She had them
typed and allowed me to read them all. I compiled a feature
programme from a selection, called it 'Letters from Abroad'
and the Home Service accepted it, with James Mageean, the
Northern Ireland drama producer in charge and Margaret D'Arcy
acting the part of Una. It was a successful production and we all
got our 'credits' – except Bob.

I have no idea how politically minded Bob was – I suspect he may have been conservative – but he was one of the few people whose politics I was not in the least interested in. It is possible to lead a useful life without being concerned with politics – though that notion I accept only with reluctance. But if I was not always concerned with an individual's politics I was always concerned with a group's, and it was Bob's fellow engineers who elected me as chairman of the local branch of our trade union, the Association of Broadcasting Staff. I thought this an honour and was proud of the post, and hope I filled it well for the three years I was elected. During this period I learned a good deal about the workings of the Corporation, and I felt that I was no longer only a member of an élite – the producers – but was also a trade unionist working actively for the material improvement of the lives of thousands of my colleagues. It was a good feeling to have, and there was a lot of work to do.

I remember two important issues. One was classified as an 'individual case' and therefore supposedly hard to negotiate for, as both parties belonged to the union. Keith Crowe, a talented studio manager, had a disagreement with one of his superiors and brought his case to the attention of the union. The union gave him little support despite my efforts on his behalf. In order to get what he considered to be the evidence necessary for his case, Keith extracted certain documents from an office and made copies of them. He was sacked as a result. He carried on with his own case, learning a good deal of law in the process. One day his lawyer remarked to him, 'You should take up the law yourself,' to which Keith replied, 'I think I will.' In the event he won his case – a surprising victory with the odds stacked against him – went on to study law at university and became a successful barrister. Many years later when I had retired from broadcasting and worked for the Lyric Theatre, Keith was engaged to fight a legal battle in which

I was involved, though not as a principal. He won this case also – I mean he won it for the side I supported.

Of what was called 'the BBC–Crowe fight' I was well acquainted with the details. The other BBC dispute, by contrast, I had nothing to do with. All I knew was that the union had backed a lightning strike in London and we in Belfast were called out in support. I was in the middle of an afternoon rehearsal for a television programme I was producing that evening, so I left the studio at once and joined a picket which a few engineers had already formed outside the front door of the BBC. It was the first and only time I was a picket, which is indicative of the sheltered industrial life I had led. Producers were conspicuous by their absence, though Rev. Moore Wasson, who was in charge of religious programmes, was conspicuous by his presence. I was not surprised to see him there because Moore, despite his quiet demeanour, was far from being a milk-and-water Christian, and could take an unpopular stance if he thought fit to do so. Indeed, his radical Presbyterianism had a good deal in common with the Presbyterians who sided with the United Irishmen in the 1798 rebellion. He and I were firm friends and I always regarded him as an ally; our sense of broadcasting values nearly always coincided. We never discussed each other's beliefs or nonbeliefs in organised religion, tacitly agreeing to respect each other's views. It was a fruitful relationship to have and we also – very important this – enjoyed the same sense of humour. Moore has divided his retirement years with teaching and preaching – a good combination – and the last time we met he told me about his work with a small congregation in Sligo. The only other ecclesiastical friendship I can claim is with Canon Eric Elliott, whom I got to know through Sam Bell before we had all settled down to marriage. Eric, like Moore, is the kind of *religieux* whose openmindedness I find stimulating; their convictions are, I think, based on a sense of certitude but they do not expect all their fellow creatures to have reached the same conclusions as themselves. Doubt is not a sin. Eric is also teaching and preaching in his retirement. His preferment has been minimal and I ca. understand why. Institutions like the various churches resemble the BBC in one respect at least: all prefer 'safe' men who will be sure never to step out of line to make trouble; and as for women, they are regarded as being admirably fitted for all sorts of jobs except those of primary importance.

One of the most unorthodox Christians I have known was Tyrone Guthrie. Guthrie never spoke of his religious beliefs – at least not to me – though when he had to express them in public he never hesitated to do so.

What I liked best was his outspokenness, for he expressed his opinions tersely and did not mind shocking his company. Once in the BBC he called 'to pay his respects' – as he put it – to a Controller whom he had known for many years. I accompanied him into the big office, where the hospitality cupboard was already open in his honour; over drinks the chat was convivial until the Controller began to recount some misdeeds in the Soviet Union.

'I detest communism and communists,' the Controller wound up vehemently.

'Really, my dear fellow. How extraordinary of you to say that,' Guthrie commented.

'Why should it be so extraordinary, Tony?'

'Oh, simply because if you were in Russia today I've no doubt you'd be a communist.'

'Don't be silly, my dear Tony. You know me too well to say that.'

'I believe it to be true,' Guthrie said quietly. 'I'm not joking.'

'I don't understand what you mean.'

'I mean you're a conformist. That's all I mean. You'd fit into any society you found yourself in, wouldn't you?'

'I don't think so.'

'Well, *I* think so. I may be a bit of a Red myself. It's possible Christ was too. What's your opinion?' he added, turning to me. 'Have you anything to say on this subject?'

I had nothing to say and the subject was changed.

'A delightful fellow, isn't he?' Guthrie said as we walked downstairs. 'Perhaps not over bright ... Well well well ... '

Guthrie was not universally admired or even liked. Who is? And no doubt he had his faults. Who has not? I remember one occasion when he allowed me to view a rehearsal he was taking in the upstairs of a Sandy Row pub. The play was *The Passing Day* by George Shiels and the rehearsal was progressing smoothly until one of the leading actors began fluffing his lines so badly that further progress was almost impossible. Suddenly Guthrie barked at the offender. 'What's the matter with you? Why don't you learn your part? You've been over it often enough. I'll stand no more of this nonsense. Go into that corner there and do some work on your lines ... I can't endure all this ... this spluttering ... Please go away!'

This was Guthrie the martinet, the schoolmaster in the classroom, the actors being his pupils, some to be encouraged with a word, a look, a gesture, others to be chided and barked at if necessary; but everything geared to his end – a successful production. In the environment of a rehearsal room – no matter how drab – Guthrie was at his best, with the cast as his adopted children, substitutes for his own childlessness, and the play, alive on the stage, his creation. I think he preferred to direct classics rather than plays by living playwrights because this gave him more latitude in interpretation – he could assume the

211

playwright's role as well as the director's and mould the play to his heart's desire.

Guthrie stayed the night with us only a month before his death. When I brought him up his breakfast I saw his ostrich legs stretched far out of the bed, and the thought struck me how awkward it must be to be six and a half feet tall and constantly having to suffer being squeezed into unsuitable beds. Guthrie forgot to pack his pyjamas when he left us, and I phoned Annaghmakerrig later in the day.

'Incinerate them, dear boy,' came his reply. 'They must be filthy.'

'Elizabeth has already washed them.'

'Oh dear. Then I suggest you bring them here the next time you agree to visit us. Are you free next week? Or the following week?'

I was not free either week and the next time I visited Annaghmakerrig was to attend Guthrie's funeral. All I learned of his death was that he had slumped over his desk one morning when he was engaged with his mail. It was, I suppose, a fitting kind of death: Guthrie never was one to make a fuss. His funeral was a quiet affair and he is buried in a country graveyard in the heart of County Monaghan, far from the metropolitan centres of England, Scotland, Canada, the United States and Australia where he spent so much of his life in the theatre.

Judith, so like him in looks and in temperament – and so overshadowed by him through all the years of their marriage – had little to live for after his death. It has been said more than once that they were more like brother and sister than man and wife. Perhaps so; but there are many different kinds of marriage. Theirs was a marriage of true minds.

11

During his BBC years I saw Bertie Rodgers frequently and sometimes without warning, so I became used to his unexpected appearances. But I was surprised one day after he had resigned from the BBC to find him standing in a queue in the Broadcasting House canteen. He joined me and said in a solemn voice, 'I've a favour to ask of you.' He then indulged in one of his long pauses to indicate the importance of his favour, so long a pause that I broke it.

'What is it, Bertie?'

'Would you be my literary executor?'

The queue moved up a pace or two and it was my turn to pause as we stood with our dangling green trays in one hand and our cutlery in the other. It seemed to me an extraordinary request to make and an extraordinary time and place to choose to make it. At last I spoke.

'I'd be honoured, Bertie, but I don't think I'd be the right person.'

'I think you are. And I've given the matter some thought.'

The queue moved forward again.

'Well, if you're certain – ' I said.

'I am.'

To mark the importance of the undertaking he drew from his pocket a copy of his booklet *Essex Roundabout* and presented it to me. It is a rare little book, published privately in Colchester, and I treasure it – though it is a second-hand copy with the first inscription carefully deleted and an inscription to me substituted: 'With respect and love from W.R. Rodgers'.

Although I had helped Bertie from time to time after he left the BBC and was trying to scrape a living as a freelance broadcaster and journalist, I found that after his death I was unable to fulfil the duties of literary executorship and Marianne, his widow, quite rightly suggested that someone else might replace me, but that meanwhile she would do what she could herself. We met a couple of times in Belfast and London to discuss possible executors, biographers and posthumous publications. She allowed me to read Bertie's private papers and dream diaries; finally and reluctantly I agreed with Marianne – though, as Bertie would have said, she did not 'put the word on it' – that I had been the wrong choice to perpetuate his literary achievement.

Still, despite my defection, Rodgers is not forgotten as man or poet and is not likely to be. Certainly his reputation has slumped in that mysterious literary stock exchange which governs such affairs: MacNeice's reputation, on the other hand, has remained steady, indeed has increased. I do not find this surprising, for MacNeice is doubtless the greater poet. Rodgers, perhaps overpraised at one time, is now undervalued and I expect his time will come again: Bertie himself was a great believer in roundabouts and swings.

Rodgers had a long final journey home to be buried. He died in the winter of 1969 in California, a misplaced man whose poetry was already out of fashion. He was sixty years old. His ashes lie in the hillside graveyard of Cloveneden, Loughgall, overlooking County Armagh. He had returned at last to the countryside where he preached as a young Presbyterian minister who might well have been an enigma to the rural flock he served. I sometimes think that MacNeice should never have beguiled him from Armagh. England could not be his home, nor America. Certainly when we met in England – whether in London or in Essex or Suffolk – we chatted mostly of Belfast, greedily exchanging gossip of our friends. Bertie was of course a great gossip; and because he was a great gossip he spent many years recording the true and the not-so-true gossip that encrusted the lives of Irish writers such as Yeats, Shaw, Joyce, Moore, Synge, Gogarty, A.E. and Higgins. If Rodgers has long been out of fashion as a poet, his book *Irish Literary Portraits* published three years after his death remains as fresh and as lively as the original radio portraits of which it is a transcript. I still read and re-read it for the insights it gives into the lives and opinions not only of some of our great Irish writers but also into the characters of their friends, some of them, like O'Connor and O'Faolain, Clarke and Colum, distinguished writers themselves. It is an undervalued book and I am very glad that I helped a little to get it published.

Like Joyce, Rodgers himself was intoxicated with words – at times perhaps too intoxicated, for his punning could pall:

Always the arriving winds of words
Pour like Atlantic gales over these ears ...

It was this poem called 'Words', along with 'Life's Circumnavigators' that Seamus Heaney chose to read at the memorial service held in First Ballymacarrett Presbyterian Church in March 1969, a few weeks after Bertie's death. Heaney was then a young poet of twenty-nine, his career just beginning, so the sense of poetic continuity gave satisfaction, I think, to many in that 'mixed' (in a religious sense) congregation. Indeed I felt that these two poets of different generations and backgrounds, one a Protestant and the other a Catholic, shared a love of words for their sounds and sources, a love of country people and the rhythms of their lives, and a love of what Ireland had been, was and perhaps might be.

I felt at home in that congregation of friends and strangers and felt too that Bertie would have been at ease in the pulpit of that familiar granite-built church just hidden from the traffic of the Albertbridge Road and the fronting nondescript Orange Hall. This gathering was in the heart of the district of Rodgers's early childhood – and of my own – and the large congregation had assembled to welcome him back home at last.

Six years before, in October 1963, I had sat at noon in the London Church of All Souls', in Langham Place, for the memorial service for Louis MacNeice. All Souls' is a beautiful church crowning the sweep of Regent Street, standing sentinel-like before the BBC. I had often passed it but never before had I entered it. Louis was not a church-going person, but if he had to have a memorial service All Souls' was certainly an appropriate church. But I was alone and felt alone, someone from Ireland in an English gathering to memorialise a man who thought of himself as Irish though by accent could be mistaken for an Englishman. I wondered what Louis would have made of it all.

On that Thursday morning, 17 October 1963, his friends filed into All Souls' and sat in silence until the service began with the sentences, 'I am the resurrection and the life, saith the Lord; he that believeth in Me, though he were dead, yet shall he live: and whosoever liveth and believeth in Me shall never die.' Then on to the *De Profundis*:

Out of the deep have I called unto thee, O Lord:
Lord, hear my voice ...

216

Then to the lesson: St Matthew 6:19–7:5

> Lay not up for yourselves treasures upon earth ...

Then Louis's own *Canzonet* was sung to the setting by Alan Rawsthorne:

> A thousand years and none the same
> Since we to light and love-light came ...

Then after the prayers we sang John Bunyan's great hymn:

> Who would true valour see
> Let him come hither;
> One here will constant be,
> Come wind, come weather ...

Then the address was delivered by W.H. Auden, his battered sauroid face visible above the pulpit, his speech measured and his praise precise and generous. This was followed by William Walton's setting of John Masefield's 'Where does the uttered music go?' Finally we sang the hymn

> All creatures of our God and King
> Lift up your voice and with us sing
> Alleluya, Alleluya.

After prayer, the organ burst into Bach's Fugue in B Minor as we filed out into the street and the everyday world.

I looked back towards Langham Place where the last straggler still stood on the steps of All Souls' but as there was no one I recognised I slowly walked away in search of a quiet café for a cup of tea and a bun – something Louis would have frowned at the very mention of, for I never had a cup of tea with him in his life; but I could not face the noisy chatter in any of his favourite pubs. I was in no mood to swop stories about his death and how premature it had been at the comparatively early age of fifty-six. 'Louis is tough,' George MacCann used to say and there was no doubt about it: Louis *was* tough. He could work hard all day and drink hard all night and rise the following day ready to absorb more punishment. His long, thin body served him well but he demanded too much from it, just as his disciplined mind served him well from his schooldays and his years at Oxford to the month of his death.

The last time I saw Louis was four months before his death when we nearly had a row. I had arranged for him to write and record a talk on his childhood in Ireland and when I arrived at his office just before two o'clock he seemed surprised to see me; Jack MacGowran, Mary Wimbush and Louis's secretary were crowded into the small office and Louis explained that he had just finished interviewing MacGowran for some programme or other.

I said reproachfully, 'Your script didn't arrive in Belfast.'

'Oh, I'm sorry about that,' he said. 'Couldn't we do it another time?'

'No, I want you to do it now.'

'But I haven't written it,' he retorted edgily.

'Well, you should have, Louis. I've studio 8B booked from two to two-thirty. It's now a quarter to two. Time to scribble a few notes on a scrap of paper and do it off the cuff.'

'I don't think I can. Let's go and have a drink first, then we'll see.' He turned towards the others, seeking their agreement, but though they were obviously in favour of a drink they knew by my tone of voice that I was displeased with Louis's cavalier attitude. 'I could give you a script next week,' he protested.

'I won't be here next week, Louis. I'll be in France on holiday from tomorrow for a fortnight. I came to London especially to record your talk.'

218

Louis saw that I was determined to have the recording made and after a sulky pause he gave way. 'Oh, very well then,' he said, adding to the others, 'I'll see you later across the road.' With a nod I followed him out of his office. My intrusion had been unpopular all round, but I was not in any mood to be concerned with that. My role was quite the opposite of Coleridge's Man from Porlock who had interrupted the inspiration of *Kubla Khan*: my intrusion as the Man from Belfast was to insist that MacNeice record 2,000 words of autobiography without preparation and with the help of a few notes he would hastily jot on a scrap of paper. Here is what he scrawled:

1st House: 2nd House; Dramatis Personae: Church and Castle: Walks: Houses: Books: Titanic and War.

That was all, and it was enough to evoke the years he spent as a child in Carrickfergus, memories which he had already written many years before and had given to Eric Dodds for safe keeping. So it was not so surprising that Louis was able to give such a fluent extempore talk, despite his reluctance to do so.

At the end of the recording he looked across the microphone at me and said, 'Well, will that do all right?'

'Yes. Exactly what I wanted.'

'What about a drink now?'

'I feel like one,' I said, and I did.

I lifted Louis's scrap of paper from the studio table and we left Broadcasting House for a pub to which the others had preceded us. We were all now in better humour.

Because Louis died so soon after this recording and because it was the only occasion we nearly quarrelled, our final meeting remains vividly in my mind. I do not regret that I bullied him into making this recording of his childhood years, and I was glad when I learned that this was the only extant recording of Louis

219

talking about his own life. It was broadcast on the Third Programme and called 'Early Memories'.

Louis' closest friends in Belfast were George and Mercy MacCann and in their picture-lined flat adjoining the Arts Theatre he was given his wake. It was a celebratory occasion and I can recall little of it except, during an interlude, a sombre chat about Louis with Hedli, his wife, when the fire had gone out of the guests and the realisation that he had left us for good sobered us up and the party was over. George had courageously made a death mask which somebody remarked was 'Louis to the life.' His ashes were now in his mother's grave in Carrowdore in the heart of County Down, a lovely old graveyard at the side of the church. But somehow, for me, Louis's ashes belong to his father's parish of St Clement's in Carrickfergus round which his earliest memories were gathered. Perhaps I am wrong in thinking that they should lie in a familiar place, for I always thought of him as a misplaced person with his restlessness, his wariness and his harsh English accent with its occasional Irish tones. Louis was a kind of fugitive figure, always on the run to somewhere else – to Iceland, America, Spain, Egypt, India, Greece.

From thirty-five years of age until sixty I put most of my energy into producing radio and television programmes. The plays for radio that I had begun to write in my spare time – original plays and adaptations of stage plays – were easy and lucrative work, but it was not really the work I wanted to do. Then I had a bit of luck. I wrote a radio play called *The Blood of Colonel Lamb*, which was rejected as being too 'controversial', a rejection which spurred me on to rewrite the play for a stage performance. This I did at once and very quickly. It was immediately accepted by the Circle Theatre in Belfast, and I at last had achieved an ambition: to have written an original stage play and had it produced. I was fifty-five years old, and beginning when most playwrights have already written a body of work and are maybe thinking of retiring.

I left the BBC in 1972 and at once experienced a sense of relief. I began to live the only life I ever wanted to live: the life of a writer. Once again, circumstances proved to be in my favour. Just as I had been appointed to the BBC at a time when regional broadcasting was expanding, so I began working in the Lyric Theatre soon after it had evolved from being a private theatre in Derryvolgie Avenue off the Malone Road – the area where Belfast's most affluent citizens lived – and resurrected itself on its present site near the King's Bridge and overlooking the River Lagan.

I became a full-time writer after a long, probably much too long, apprenticeship. It seemed a ridiculous undertaking – to become a dramatist at an age when I should be taking life easy; but it never struck me to give up my ambition because of age. I had almost perfect health, a pension, a grown-up family, a quiet house, a room for work, and a new theatre willing to engage my services. Everything seemed to fall into place to my advantage according to a predestined plan. Sometimes I think my life resembles a well-made play. But the final act is not yet over.

OTHER TITLES
from
BLACKSTAFF PRESS

DUTCH INTERIOR
FRANK O'CONNOR

'Moonlight streamed down in a narrow cone and expanded in a corner of the whitewashed wall. Ned tossed restlessly and drew his hands through his hair ...

"Bloody old fools!" he whispered savagely. "Fear is the one thing in their lives – fear, fear, fear. Fear of this world or fear of the next. 'What'll become of us?' 'What'll the neighbours say?' 'You can't do this and you can't do that.' " '

Intimate and truthful, Frank O'Connor's portrayal of Irish provincial life has made him one of the most influential and respected of modern writers. But it was this same searching honesty that caused the censorship of his work by the Irish government in the 1940s and 1950s.

Banned on its publication in 1940, *Dutch Interior* is striking for the integrity of its account of the effects of Catholic conservatism and sexual repression on a group of young men and women growing up in Cork city. As they fall in love, marry, emigrate or become trapped by their own pasts, O'Connor traces their changing fortunes with characteristic humour and sensitivity. And in its insight into the 'flash points of human experience', this novel is a forceful reminder of his unique talent.

'Every word has to be read.'
New Republic

'Frank O'Connor is a master of prose.'
Irish Times

198 x 129 mm; 304 pp; 0-85640-432-2; pb;

£4.95

THE SAINT AND MARY KATE
FRANK O'CONNOR

Sharing the hardships of life in a Cork slum tenement,
Mary Kate McCormick and Phil 'the Saint' Dinan become
firm childhood friends. The years pass, and Phil lives up to
his nickname by becoming excessively pious; meanwhile
Mary Kate blossoms into a passionate young woman. And
then things start to get a little complicated – for Mary Kate
has more than friendship in mind ...

Delightful in its account of the vagaries of unrequited love,
Frank O'Connor's *The Saint and Mary Kate* is a touching
study of friendship and an engaging look at the struggle
between the world of the spirit and the world of the flesh.

'O'Connor is a serious artist and observer'
Irish Times

198 x 129 mm; 304 pp; 0-85640-445-4; pb

£4.95

HONOUR THY FATHER
EAMONN MC GRATH

'We walked back silently in the still evening. Already the
first dew was light on the grass, moistening our toecaps to
dullness. There was a new easiness between us, an
understanding that had no need of words to define and
circumscribe it. Inside me, rising like a lark on a bright
pillar of air, my spirits soared and sang. The sky out over
the islands was still warm with memory of day. A croak of
crows, tumbling home to roost, passed overhead, buoyant
in the free drift of air. And, over all, the elemental singing
in my head. My father had recognised my individuality,
my right to be myself, to carve my own destiny out of the
unique piece of life that was me.'

Set in County Wexford, *Honour Thy Father* is a graceful and
honest study of a growing child's experience of Irish rural
life. Mc Grath explores familiar subject material – a loveless
marriage, provincial small-mindedness, boarding school
brutality, adolescent sexuality and first love – but breathes
new life and vigour into it through his startling freshness
of expression and insight.

Centring on the young John Foley's gradually heightening
awareness of the complexities and hidden truths of family
life, *Honour Thy Father* is a powerful portrait of a son's
struggle for a deeper and more compassionate connection
with his father.

'A study of a classic Irish boyhood ... a quiet and
truthful book'
Claire Tomalin, *Observer*

'Its climate almost Dickensian, soaked in the aroma
of country pubs'
Martin Levin, *New York Times*

198 x 129 mm; 256 pp; 0-85640-433-0; pb

£4.95

THE CHARNEL HOUSE

EAMONN MC GRATH

Set in Ardeevan sanatorium in the 1950s, when tuberculosis was still a major cause of death in Ireland, *The Charnel House* is a powerful study of the twilight existence of the chronically and terminally ill.

Bringing together a wide and varied set of characters – Richard Cogley and his sister Eileen, young lovers Vincent and Lily, the eccentric Commander Barnwell, hospital joker Arty Byrne, homosexual Phil Turner, and the embittered Frank O'Shea – Eamonn Mc Grath charts their relationships as they confront pain and death, creating a deeply felt examination of the nature of suffering and the unexpected strength of the human spirit.

198 x 129 mm; 224 pp; 0-85640-447-0; pb

£5.95

MY COUSIN JUSTIN

MARGARET BARRINGTON

'As I watched my husband and my cousin, I realized
for the first time that ... each was as badly
mutilated as if he had lost an arm or leg. What they
had lost was more because one could not see it. The
scars of war lay on their souls, and old wounds
ache.'

When Loulie Delahaie moves from the shelter of
her Anglo-Irish upbringing in County Donegal, and
the claustrophobic intensity of her relationship
with her cousin Justin Thorauld, she finds herself
embroiled in the merciless world of Dublin
journalism and revolutionary politics. There she is
swept into a headlong love affair with Egan
O'Doherty, a gunman on the run from
the Black and Tans.

The bitter violence of the Irish Civil War and the
dark shadows it casts over Loulie, Justin and Egan
are powerfully caught in this absorbing story of
passion and deceit.

'Seldom are landscape, atmosphere, characters made so
clear with such untroubled ease – the words flow as
easily on the pages as water.'
New York Herald Tribune

'a novel of great delicacy, beauty and subtlety'
Washington Post

198 x 129 mm; 288 pp; 0-85640-456-X; pb

£4.95

THE HOLLOW BALL

SAM HANNA BELL

'He should have known that McFall's subversive concern
with these men who went through life as ciphers would
grow and swell in the back streets. And he felt no shame in
regarding himself as different from them ... He was going,
by right, to where men paid honourably and handsomely
for his considerable skill. He stared back coldly at the
heavy face of his companion.'

Trapped in their poorly paid menial jobs in a clothing firm,
David Minnis and Bonar McFall both yearn for a better life.
McFall is angered by the injustice he sees around him and
seeks change through radical politics; Minnis dreams of
becoming a star footballer and dedicates his life to the
pursuit of 'the hollow ball'. When he is signed by
Glenbank Athletic, his life changes dramatically. Success
breeds success, but also compromise and betrayal,
gradually alienating Minnis from his family and friends.

Painting a haunting picture of working-class Belfast in the
1930s – where men and women 'fight like dogs for an extra
twopence an hour' – this novel from the author of *December
Bride* is a poignant study of the tragic price that is paid for
fame.

'... told skilfully, calmly, and at times beautifully ... Bell has
given us a vivid and accurate portrayal of working-class
Protestant people.'
Brian Friel, *Irish Times*

'... has no truck with the journalese and sensationalism that often
characterize fiction about sport.'
Times Literary Supplement

198 x 129 mm; 256 pp; 0-85640-452-7; pb

£4.95

December Bride

Sam Hanna Bell

'a story of the eternal triangle, held, like the land, by
stubborn force'
Fortnight

THE CLASSIC NOVEL OF ULSTER LIFE, NOW A MAJOR FILM.

Sarah Gomartin, the servant girl on Andrew Echlin's farm,
bears a child to one of Andrew's sons. But which one? Her
steadfast refusal over many years to 'bend and contrive
things' by choosing one of the brothers reverberates
through the puritan Ulster community, alienating clergy
and neighbours, hastening her mother's death and casting
a cold shadow on the life of her children.

December Bride, directed by Thaddeus O'Sullivan and
starring Saskia Reeves, Donal McCann and Ciaran Hinds,
was ecstatically received at its première at the 1990
Dublin Film Festival.

'not just a remarkable artistic achievement, but also a remarkable
political one ... opens up a community's sense of itself, restoring
a richness and complexity to a history that has been deliberately
narrowed'
Fintan O'Toole, *Irish Times*, reviewing
the film *December Bride*

198 x 129 mm; 304 pp; 0-85640-061-0; pb

£4.95

CASTLE CORNER
JOYCE CARY

'The crowd, now gathered close, watched in silence the
bailiffs fetch rakes, poles, and a long-handled pruning
hook, but when they approached Con's new-built cabin
and began to hook down the roof, there were sudden yells
of "Give them Martin, up the League."
'Martin was a district inspector of police murdered the
year before.
'Old John gazed round with an air of mild reproach; John
Chass, looking embarrassed, smiled and attempted a joke;
the D.I., with a marble face but very brisk legs, walked up
and down in front of the police, who looked like men
awaiting the dentist, some with resignation, some with
ferocious resolution.'

Violent evictions in Donegal, fashionable drawing-rooms in
London, compromise and degradation in a West African
trading station – Joyce Cary's panoramic novel follows the
fortunes of the Anglo-Irish Corner family as they contend
with a changing world at the century's turn.

'Mr Cary's book is stupendous ... There is an intellectual
richness ... pages of allusive anecdote, chat, picture, narrative,
family history, and a grim display of human squalor ... It is a
grand effect; and the book has a fury of incontrovertible detail.'
Frank Swinnerton, *Observer*

198 x 129 mm; 432 pp; 0-85640-422-5; pb

£5.95

NO SURRENDER
ROBERT HARBINSON

'The event was spectacular. Nearly eleven pounds I weighed. "Ya've the muscles of a man," said the district nurse when she congratulated Big 'Ina on having such a brute. My mother never forgot the nurse's remark. The years that followed were to prove that only those muscles would ensure our survival.'

Robert Harbinson's famous account of his Belfast boyhood – the devastating shock of his window-cleaner father's early death, his mother Big 'Ina's unending battles against poverty and tuberculosis ('It' to the little family), his first rapturous encounters with nature, circumscribed as it was by 'the Bog Meadows' marshy steppes' – was enthusiastically received when it was first published in 1960.

'A tough, but never a hard-luck tale Mr Harbinson manages to make his; full of pathos and pride and fresh, hot anger. . . [he] makes us believe in the passions of his childhood.'
Guardian

'He is on all planes at once; humorous, detailed and objective as a Brueghel village scene; quietly indignant over injustices practised by the toffs; puzzled, exploratory, expectant, as a growing boy. . . He writes as one with a true sense of poetry.'
The Times

'. . . crammed with the stuff of life. The raucous cobbled streets, the grimy mission halls and the evening mists that made the Bog Meadows a place of mystery, the bitterness and the passion of the religious and political background – Robert Harbinson conjures them up out of his memory with a sureness of touch that gives authority to every page.'
Irish Independent

First paperback edition

198 x 129 mm; 224 pp; 0 85640 383 0; pb
£4.50

ORDERING BLACKSTAFF BOOKS

All Blackstaff Press books are available through bookshops. In the case of difficulty, however, orders can be made directly to the publisher. Indicate clearly the title and number of copies required and send order with your name and address to:

CASH SALES

Blackstaff Press Limited
3 Galway Park
Dundonald
Belfast BT16 0AN
Northern Ireland

Please enclose a remittance to the value of the cover price plus: £1.00 for the first book plus 60p per copy for each additional book ordered to cover postage and packing. Payment should be made in sterling by UK personal cheque, postal order, sterling draft or international money order, made payable to Blackstaff Press Limited.

Applicable only in the UK and Republic of Ireland
Full catalogue available on request